Working with Universities

How businesses & universities can work together profitably

Adam Jolly

crimson

Working with Universities

Published in Great Britain in 2011 by
Crimson Publishing Ltd
Westminster House
Kew Road
Richmond
Surrey
TW9 2ND

A catalogue record for this book is available from the British Library.

ISBN 978 1 85458 687 2

The information contained within *Working with Universities* is of a general nature and, as such, is not intended to address the circumstances of any particular individual or entity. While every effort has been made to provide accurate and timely information, there can be no guarantee that it will continue to be accurate when it is received or in the future. Appropriate professional advice should be sought after a thorough examination of the particular situation.

No responsibility can be accepted by the author or the publisher for loss or damage occasioned to any business acting on or refraining from action, as a result of the material in this book.

Typeset by Mac Style, Nafferton, East Yorkshire
Printed and bound in the UK by Ashford Colour Press, Gosport, Hants

Contents

Contents

Contents

Foreword

In searching for future value in the economy as a whole and in your business in particular, universities are playing an ever more central role as pioneers on the frontlines of knowledge and as trainers of the next generation of talent.

To these twin academic pillars of research and education, a third is being added. Enterprise. Not as a bolt-on. Not as a nod to the powers that be. But as an integral part of the role that universities now play and the impact that they make.

This elevation has happened gradually over the last 20 years. It is a new language that everyone is learning how to speak and not everyone can express it as clearly as they would like. But enterprise in all its dimensions is now ready to play a leading part in how universities evolve in the highly competitive, open economy in which we now find ourselves.

Internally, it finds expression in two main ways: backing the rising tide of graduates who are creating their own businesses; and capitalising on all that has been learnt about how to find commercial applications for research through licences and spin-outs.

As well as finding their own way to market, universities are becoming an integral part of the wider innovation system, supporting ventures at each stage of their efforts to become one of the big businesses of tomorrow.

These external engagements are by no means limited to formal research programmes and recruitment at the end of the summer term. Through their knowledge transfer offices, the universities are creating numerous tools for smaller enterprises, many of which are supported by grant funding.

As an entrepreneur, you can test your ideas, explore your options, bring in bright sparks on short-term assignments, improve your skills at work, ask for a perspective from an expert, sharpen up your processes, buy in a technique, have your software rewritten, join a network of those active in your field, bid for grants to fund your growth or open up sources of capital.

In running such programmes and collaborations, universities will retain their own distinct identity with their own set of educational priorities. But in a real and exciting sense, they are becoming magnets for enterprises, around which clusters of knowledge, talent and capital are starting to flourish.

As a route to growth, universities now offer options which are worth exploring by any business, so I welcome the publication of this title which seeks to explain and illustrate how the relationship between the two can best work.

Allyson Reed
Director of Enterprise and Communications
Technology Strategy Board
November 2011

Acknowledgements

This book draws on the experience, expertise, inspiration and commitment of those who have put so much into realising the potential for collaboration between those at the forefront of knowledge and those who know how to take ideas to market.

I am particularly grateful to everyone at the Technology Strategy Board, the Intellectual Property Office, PraxisUnico, Universities UK, Interface, Auril, the Higher Education Funding Council for England and Research Councils UK for their generosity and patience in giving me their input and guidance. In combination, it is a powerful machine being created to help turn knowledge and talent into commercial reality.

I was also fortunate to speak to many of the most active and influential participants in the innovative space that lies between universities and the market. I would like to thank all those in knowledge transfer offices, business incubators, enterprise centres, careers offices, funding agencies and innovation labs who were happy to straighten out my thinking and point me in the right direction.

In particular, Douglas Robertson at Newcastle University ran me through how the business of technology transfer has grown. On a tour round the Coventry campus in the snow, Brian More gave me an insight into how universities are now supporting and accommodating entrepreneurs and innovators. Garrick Jones of Ludic, London School of Economics and the Royal College of Art and Design, Bruce Girvan at Ceres Power, Maxine Horn at Creative Barcode and Margaret Henry at Oxford Innovation all brought me up to speed on how innovation is now evolving as a discipline. Tony Walker at Manchester University was happy to open some fascinating doors in one of Europe's leading centres for technology and Simon Roodhouse at the Institute of Work Based Learning made some invaluable comments on the role of universities in fostering talent throughout someone's career. Chris Rigby at Robert Gordon, Frank Couling at Bedfordshire, Ian Brotherston at Heriot-Watt, Alan Burbidge at Nottingham, Louise O'Neill at Glasgow, Charles Hancock at Derby, Peter Shearer at Aston and Tom Hockaday at Oxford were all remarkably helpful in shedding light on different ways in which smaller companies can engage with universities. I would also like to thank Simon Bond at Bath Ventures, Mark Thompson at Carbon First, Ederyn Williams at Warwick Ventures, Hina Wadhwa-Gonfreville and Dawn Bournand at QS, David Way at the Technology Strategy Board, and Lisa Redman at the Intellectual Property Office for their excellent editorial contributions.

On the other side of the equation, I have drawn wherever possible on the insights of entrepreneurs and executives based on their experience of running projects with universities. As always, it is easy to overlook the risks and the challenges that such innovators run in taking ideas to market. My hope is that their business sense is reflected in how this book has been structured and written.

Acknowledgements

Finally, I am grateful to everyone at Crimson Publishing for their faith and commitment in this project. The story of how universities fit into the challenge of growing a business has been a fascinating one to tell. It is a plot that is set to continue unfolding dynamically, I am sure, so I would be interested in any comments you have on what has happened so far and what might happen next. You are welcome to email me at adamjolly@aol.com.

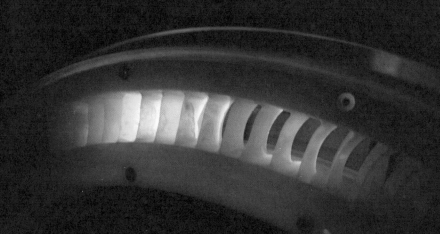

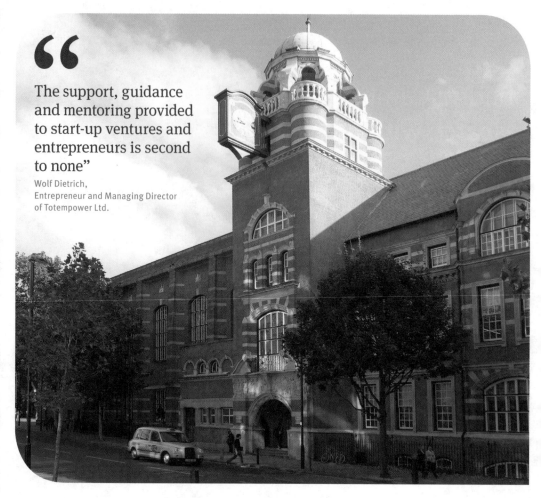

PART 1
Growth potential

HELP YOUR BUSINESS EXPAND

INVEST IN A WEALTH OF TALENT

We're dedicated to providing businesses with access to talented, industry-ready graduates. Just ask some of our friends at Apple, *Cartier* and Cisco.

UPGRADE
YOUR
FUTURE

BIRMINGHAM
CITY
University

Visit **www.bcu.ac.uk/business** or call **0121 331 5252** to learn more about our range of services for all businesses from research and consultancy to partnerships, knowledge transfer and training

1

The value of universities to entrepreneurs

An introduction to the services and expertise universities can offer SMEs

Pete Higgins was making a sandwich for his son. Should he add some mayonnaise, he wondered? When exactly had he opened the jar though? Could it still be eaten? If it was just him, he would probably have put this doubts aside and tucked in. Because it was his son, he chucked out the mayo.

Surely, he thought, there had to be a better way of tracking the date by when you had to eat food. What on earth must it cost if we all end up behaving like he did?

Actually, as he subsequently found, it adds up to £11bn in wasted food in the UK every year and is a problem retailers and major brands have voluntarily been trying to crack together since 2006. As no-one else seemed to be doing much to create a smart label about when to "use within", Higgins decided to give it a go himself.

As a non-scientist, who had trained as an architect and run a digital media agency for 10 years, he asked a number of universities to produce feasibility studies to test out his ideas, looking at the potential for electronic and chemical solutions. Up until Easter 2010, the venture he had formed, UWI (Use Within) Technology, had produced some interesting but uneconomic results, so remained on hold.

The breakthrough came when he came across the right academic and the right commercial officer at Heriot-Watt University in Edinburgh. Their research into micro fluids opened up the potential for Higgins to change the colour on labels as they approached their sell-by date by transferring chemicals through channels of less than a hundredth of a millimetre in a diameter.

Funded in part by an innovation voucher of £5,000, Higgins commissioned two projects: one to trigger the flow of chemicals when you opened the lid and the other to control the speed at which the switch from green to red happened. Food might perish after a week in the fridge, but he was also hoping to produce a version for cosmetics and medicines which last a year on the shelf.

So far, UWI is only making test labels in the university lab. The next stage is to produce a working model for potential customers, which will be produced through another project run with the university. The university is recruiting a researcher for a year, who will then transfer to UWI.

After spending £50,000 in developing his ideas, Higgins, now 46, has the credibility to start attracting more outside funds for the business. As well as a SMART award for £70,000 from Scottish Enterprise to fund the development of a manufacturing

UWI (Use Within) Technology

model, a private investor has put in £50,000 for a 2.3% stake and UWI received £50,000 from Barclays as the winner of its competition, "Take one small step".

For Higgins, the plan is to sell licences to all the different sectors which could use the labels and to be making profits of £8m within five years.

For other enterprises, universities can be equally valuable partners not just in creating breakthroughs and innovations, but in making improvements and finding fixes. Through the university, you can gain access to the combination of knowledge, talent, funding, networks and space that you need to grow.

Access to knowledge

Academic researchers are on the frontline of knowledge. They are asking the questions and making the discoveries that are going to create future value within the economy.

The timelines on which they are working may well be too extended for you. But academics also have the expertise within their field to lay out all the options and point you in the right direction to sort out your challenges in real time.

Even in a medium-sized research university, you will find a thousand academics working on nearly all aspects of human endeavour. Science. Commerce. Design. Digital media. Put the right question to the right academic and you will get a rigorous answer that can lift your whole business.

You might be surprised by the enthusiasm of the response from experts who are going to see their technology appear in the real world for the first time. Pete Higgins said: "They are excited because micro fluids have never been used in labels or timing devices before and could now sell in millions of products around the world."

The chances of having such a meaningful dialogue are improving all the time. Over the last 10 years, universities have put in place mechanisms to handle projects of all sizes. Like UWI, you can start with short, initial studies and build up into more ambitious collaborations. At each point, the university's commercial transfer officer is there to act as your translator.

Access to talent

In attracting the best minds to answer the toughest questions, universities act as another source of competitive advantage for smaller companies: training graduates in the high-level scientific, commercial and creative skills on which future economic performance is going to depend.

Universities are developing a more flexible set of mechanisms for smaller enterprises to access that talent. Alongside traditional recruitment, you can bring in graduates on internships and placements at any point in the year, not just at the end of the summer term. Or, like UWI, you can run joint research projects with a view to recruiting a graduate once you have finished. That way, you can prove your concept first, as well as seeing whether your potential recruit can make the switch to the commercial world.

Access to funding

This flow of knowledge and talent into the economy is becoming central to public policy. Universities are becoming leading players in supporting business regionally and nationally. They are often able to draw on public funds to make different forms of collaboration happen.

Many, for instance, run innovation vouchers worth between £3,000 and £5,000 to encourage initial projects between universities and SMEs. All are heavily engaged in placing graduates within business to pursue innovative projects, saving you two-thirds of the normal cost. Most can advise you on how to set up a collaboration in such a way to draw on national or European schemes. Some enterprises are even participating in funded consortiums as a way of driving their growth.

As well as public funds, the commercial teams at universities, particularly those in enterprise and innovation centres, have good links with local networks of investors or may even be running their own funds. Alongside such equity, more and more are looking to turn it into "smart money" by bringing in coaches and advisers to keep your plan on track.

Platforms for growth

Such proximity to those in the know can make all the difference in launching an innovation and it is no coincidence that as part of its development, UWI has just moved to a science park within five minutes of Heriot-Watt. It puts them in a good position to keep bouncing ideas off the research team, as well as staying in touch with the commercial office.

Many universities now offer space to ventures under their wing with a view to letting them grow flexibly. Usually, these are accompanied by a business advisory service. You can start as a virtual tenant, before taking a desk or a room in an incubator. Once you scale up, you can then move to offices at the innovation centre and even run operations on a business park.

Whether or not you are located on campus, you can keep yourself in the flow of ideas, look for solutions and spot potential candidates by joining any one of a number of business-to-academic networks. Your local university will be able to plug you into anything relevant. At the national level, a series of specialist networks are run through the Technology Strategy Board, which you are free to join.

As well as their traditional role in mapping out the future, universities are becoming an integral part of what anyone in business can achieve today. Looking back at the last 18 months, since the start of his work with Heriot-Watt, Higgins says: "I can't stress enough how positive and forward-looking the university were. I might be a non-scientist, but we have verified the idea and have the research on which to build."

The UK's universities in numbers

- The UK has a total of 165 higher education institutions (HEIs) of which 115 are universities and the rest are colleges and institutes.

- In total, HEIs have an output of £59bn a year, generating more for the UK economy than sectors such as pharmaceuticals, agriculture or advertising (from the report *The impact of universities on the UK economy*, produced for Universities UK by Ursula Kelly, Donald McLellan and Professor Iain McNicoll of the University of Strathclyde in 2009).

- The UK has 11 universities in the world's top 100, a figure second only to the US (quoted by Higher Education Funding Council for England (HEFCE), 2011).

- Research productivity in the UK's universities is the world's highest, resulting in more publications and citations per pound spent than anywhere else (quoted by HEFCE, 2011).

- In 2009–10, there were 2.5 million students attending British universities, a 60% increase in the 15 years since 1994/95 (UK Universities).

- The teaching model in universities will undergo fundamental change in 2012, as £2.9bn is removed from the £7.1bn resource budget for higher education and the cap on student fees rises from £3,000 to £9,000.

- In the government's spending review, funding for science and research has been given strategic priority and is being frozen at £4.6bn a year until 2014–15 (Department for Business Innovation and Skills, 2010).

- The Higher Education Innovation Fund has confirmed that it will continue to put £150m a year into building up the capacity within universities to transfer knowledge into real-world applications through to 2014–15.

- In 2003, less than 20% of business had links with HEIs, by 2010 it had risen to 66%, according to the CBI.

- 48% of SMEs consider that universities have changed their culture in the last 10 years to be more commercial and business-facing, but 55% would like a clearer idea of who to approach about the potential for collaborating (survey on engagement between SMEs and higher education institutes, Institute of Directors and Universities UK, 2011).

- The UK's universities are earning a total of £3bn a year from their commercial activities in exchanging knowledge, a figure which has been growing at 6% a year since 2003 (Department for Business Innovation and Skills, 2010).

- More than 2.5m new connections were made between experts and innovators through Knowledge Transfer Networks in 2009.

- Nearly 1,000 businesses were part of a Knowledge Transfer Partnership with a university in 2009. Small businesses with between 10 and 50 employees were the most engaged, representing 37% of the total.

Expert comment by Ederyn Williams, Warwick Ventures

Academics, explorers and entrepreneurs

"Why don't you come out of your ivory tower and see what the real world is like?" say the hard-nosed businessmen to the academics.

But in today's fast moving environment, we don't just need to know what the world is like now, but what it will become. Academics, especially in science, engineering and medicine, are often explorers of future possibilities. Developing the economy of the future requires new discoveries, new technologies, and new business opportunities.

In Warwick Ventures, we have the privilege of working with these explorers, who develop new and exciting opportunities. Of course, some won't work. And some may be too far ahead of their time. But many offer great potential, if only our explorers could meet and work with the entrepreneurs who could take their promising ideas forward.

Businesses, especially small ones in hard times, often have very short time horizons. Surviving until next year can be a real challenge: thinking about an innovation that might become a product in a decade seems like a luxury. Fortunately, there are many who realise that their future prosperity requires that they understand the next generation of products, and are willing to work with universities such as Warwick to discover these.

But sometimes we can't find such an existing company to license our technology to. The Google story is illustrative. When Sergey Brin and Larry Page invented their new search engine, the Stanford University technology transfer office tried to help them to license it. Yahoo weren't interested; Lycos offered $750,000, but it was judged to be too little. So they raised enough money from friends and family to start their own company and the rest is history.

This is often the reason for a university spin-out company: it's the only way to move the technology forward into the market. Such companies have terrible growing pains, as they start with nothing, but thankfully there are many brave entrepreneurs and investors who are willing to have a go. Many new IP-based companies (often called 'spin-outs') fail, but 40% or more can survive and prosper, and the occasional one becomes enormously successful, changes an entire industry and makes lots of money for everyone involved.

In the 1990s, university technology transfer was all about making money. Now, we are also trying to change the world. And as Ross Perot said: "Most new jobs won't come from our biggest employers. They will come from our smallest. We've got to do everything we can to make entrepreneurial dreams a reality."

Ederyn Williams founded Warwick Ventures in April 2000. It has the mission of commercialising the world-leading research of the university, in which £120m per year is invested. Warwick Ventures works with many individuals and commercial partners, who collaborate in product development, invest in spin-out companies and license technologies.

2

How universities have changed

Universities are transforming the ways they capture knowledge and talent to create innovations

Brian Steele thought he might be onto a winner. As a professor at Imperial College London, then as now, one of the powerhouses of British engineering, he sensed his latest idea in conducting technology could well appeal to the electronics industry.

In 1980, he filed a patent in the hope of finding a buyer for his licence. No-one showed any interest. The only alternative, he was advised, was to sell up. The only taker was one of the leading American players who bought the rights in his lithium iode for $1,000, then put it at the heart of a series of computer chips that sold in their millions.

Back then, as Bruce Girvan, a graduate from the business school at Imperial and subsequently a colleague of Steele, explains: "The thought of creating a company purely on a patent really wasn't in the European psyche and certainly not among academics."

In a way, Steele's experience was part of a gloriously inventive, if financially foolhardy, British tradition. Take penicillin, one of the greatest scientific breakthroughs of the 20th or any other century. It was discovered by Alexander Fleming in the late 1920s. Yet whose lives did it save in the Second World War? Mainly American.

Like many of his academic peers, Fleming laudably believed that science was a public good. By claiming any exclusivity in penicillin, he was worried about preventing its use for the benefit of all. The trouble was that it left no economic base for developing the drug.

Instead, it was left to American pharmaceutical companies to apply for patents and bring the drug into general production, subsequently saving the lives of thousands of soldiers, sailors and airmen.

It would be good to say that there were no other examples of discoveries that were made here, but turned into commercial reality elsewhere, but the public-spirited, enlightened pursuit of pure science is strong within universities. No-one could question the brilliance and commitment of British academic research, but the commercial scope for capitalising on all their accumulated knowledge to create the big businesses of tomorrow was often left unfulfilled.

As Dr Mike Lynch, the founder and chief executive of Autonomy, and a graduate who took an IT start-up onto the FTSE 100 before recently selling it to Hewlett Packard for $7bn, said:

> *"If you look around Cambridge, the companies have great technology and poor marketing. In Silicon Valley it's often the other way around. It's a question of putting the two together. We all like to think that the best technology wins, but the realisation that marketing is so important can be a bitter blow."*

For Brian Steele and Imperial at least, the chance came to make amends. By the late 1990s, he was developing his next big idea of using ceramics in a fuel cell. In his patent, he set out a complete system for injecting fuel and air to extract power and heat. It created the potential for letting us run our own little low-carbon generators in a cupboard at home, heating the house and water as normal, then giving us electricity for free.

As a design patent, it represented a completely new chemical technology. Neither Steele nor Imperial were going to sell themselves short this time. A new company, Ceres Power, was created as a spin-out in 2001 and £4.25m was raised. In 2004, a further £15.9m was raised through an AIM flotation and British Gas bought a 10% share for £20m in 2008. The first fuel cells are being installed next year.

Originally recruited to write the business plan, Bruce Girvan is now director of innovation at the company.

> "To prove our fuel cell worked, we were going to need a lot of investment. An enormous amount of engineering sits around Brian's fuel cell. In countries like Japan, it is accepted that it will take years to develop a complex technology to the point of manufacture. Our view was that we wanted to be a global plc from the start, so we had to hit it hard."

The scale of ambition at Ceres might be unusual, but the experience is not. Over the last 20 years, British universities have been on an extraordinary journey to learn how best to capture the value in their knowledge and talent.

They have moved into a different dimension, says Allyson Reed, director of enterprise and communications at the Technology Strategy Board.

> "You just used to start in the lab, then find someone to take the research to market. If you managed to pass the baton, you might eventually create a hot product. Universities are now more fully part of the innovation system. As well as being a source of bright ideas and different thinking, they are also becoming a magnet for collaboration and talent. As a business, you can find yourself being absorbed into a cluster of like-minded enterprises, where you can build up networks and find the right skills.
>
> After the experience of the last 20 years, the UK appears to many to be the gold standard. National commissions in both Canada and Germany are looking at us in their search for answers in how to turn new technologies into high-growth ventures."

There is no place for complacency in how we commercialise technology, she says. "It is like learning a language. We might now be getting the gist, but we have a long way to go until we speak it really well."

In most universities, a mechanism to bring order and structure to their relations with business has only been in place for the last 10 years. Before, even leading research universities such as Southampton, only had a single industrial liaison officer.

Since then the Higher Education Innovation Fund (HEIF) has put millions into developing a professional capability to cover all aspects of collaboration. As a result, over 30 people now work at Southampton specialising in areas such as research partnerships, contract negotiations, consultancy, licensing and spin-outs.

Originally known as technology transfer, these activities were designed to prevent ideas slipping through the net and to encourage academics to put forward ideas on the right terms. The effective management of intellectual property is fundamental, of course. No business can take the results of any research to market without being sure about the degree of exclusivity it can claim.

The original hopes that the effective management of IP would lead to a steady stream of income for universities have largely proved misplaced. Raw technology is never easy to bring to market. It is a complex, unpredictable and expensive task. Returns mostly come from the occasional, one-off hit.

Universities remain firmly committed to the overall process of knowledge transfer for two reasons. First, high-growth ventures often come from the most unlikely sources. Second, to prove the value of their research and to engage their students, universities have to make sure that their activities have an impact in the real world. From 2014, this commitment will be reflected in their research grants, accounting for 20% of any assessment, alongside more traditional academic measures.

To reflect this wider remit, commercial activities within the universities are now generally defined as knowledge transfer or even as knowledge exchange. Alongside IP, which produces a legally defined snapshot of an idea, the softer sources of know-how and expertise that lie behind these hard rights can be just as valuable. It is a question of how to tap into all the brainpower and experience that has accumulated in the head of someone who is on the frontline of knowledge in your field.

For enterprises, it brings two particular schemes into play: Knowledge Transfer Partnerships (KTPs) and Knowledge Transfer Networks (KTNs).

1. **KTPs** are funded schemes for up-and-coming academics to work on-site to solve a challenge within a business. They can be a powerful stimulant. One maker of caravans in East Yorkshire took its sales up from £6m to £20m by bringing in engineers from the University of Hull when moving into the market for holiday lodges.

2. **KTNs** are designed for innovation in an economy where knowledge is more freely available and circulates more quickly than ever before. Particularly as a small company, you can no longer afford to operate in isolation. By joining a network, you can follow developments, source ideas and find experts, putting you on a fast track to finding solutions and building collaborative partnerships.

The attractions of KTNs are equally strong for universities. In a report titled *The Edgeless University* for the progressive think tank Demos, Peter Bradwell argues:

"Technology is changing universities as they become just one source among many for ideas, knowledge and innovation. Collaborative online tools that allow people to work together more easily and open access to content are both the cause of change and a tool with which they can respond."

In reviewing the role of universities, Bradwell predicts:

"It is no longer contained within the campus, nor within the physically defined space of a particular institution, nor, sometimes, even in higher education institutions at all ... it is driven by people finding new ways to access and use ideas and knowledge, by new networks of learning and innovation, and by collaborative research networks that span institutions and businesses."

In the past, he says, competitive advantages might have lain with those who had the resources on the ground in the form of infrastructure and commodities. Today what matters is who has the skills, the ideas, the insights and the creativity. Universities will be valued as stores of knowledge capital, he argues, providing space for developing the expertise and validating the learning on which the economy is going to depend.

Expert comment by the Technology Strategy Board

Knowledge Transfer Partnerships

Part-funded by the government, Knowledge Transfer Partnerships (KTP) is Europe's leading programme helping businesses to improve their competitiveness, productivity and performance through collaboration and knowledge transfer between business and academia.

In a Knowledge Transfer Partnership, a business teams up with a further or higher education institution to work on a specific innovation project for six to 18 months. In this partnership, an 'Associate' (typically a recently qualified graduate or someone who has completed post-doctoral research) plays a key role in managing and implementing tactical or strategic development in the business and transferring knowledge between the business and the knowledge base.

In 2007, the Technology Strategy Board took over the management of the programme, working closely with the other co-funding organisations to maintain the successful record of KTPs. This is demonstrated by the fact that more than 5,000 organisations have been realising the benefits of the programme since its inception more than 35 years ago.

It has been estimated that on average, a KTP project increases annual profit (before tax) by £284,000, creating three new jobs and resulting in 29 business staff being trained. Typically, the project also leads to three new research projects being initiated and an average of £114,000 invested in new plant and machinery. The following examples illustrate the range of completed projects funded under the KTP programme.

- **Orangebox Ltd:** designs and manufactures commercial furniture. Recognising that, to remain competitive, it had to become even more efficient and responsive to customer requirements, the company turned to Cardiff University as its partner in a KTP project to develop a new manufacturing paradigm that has improved lead times with associated cost savings of £600,000.

- **The Cutty Sark Trust:** the independent charity responsible for the conservation, maintenance and display of the world's only surviving tea clipper. After a report predicted the ship would fall apart within 10 years, the Trust turned to the University of Greenwich to collaborate on a KTP to transfer finite element Analysis (FEA) skills and technology to predict how components would behave in renovation scenarios. The project's results supported the Trust's successful submission to the Heritage Lottery Fund, resulting in £13m towards the ship's conservation.

- **Breval Environmental Limited:** working with Bell College (now part of the University of West Scotland), it developed a self-propelled vehicle for coating, cleaning and maintaining ducting systems, leading to the company being presented with the Royal Society of Engineering "Best Engineering Excellence" Award for the project.

These case studies show that one of the key strengths of KTPs is that they are open to any size of organisation from any sector – commercial, public sector and not-for-profit – supported by the best academic knowledge and expertise.

Expert comment by Alice Frost, Higher Education Funding Council for England

Knowledge exchange: unlocking university expertise

What is knowledge exchange?

Many university subjects – from engineering, science, social science and business through to art and design – have relevance to business. Knowledge and expertise in universities can help with product and process innovations in businesses, as well as organisational design, branding and marketing, and professional development for enterprise and innovation.

Universities have long recognised that knowledge and research developed through higher education (HE) have value for businesses and economic growth as well as for wider society, such as for health or culture. This started originally with technology transfer, licensing university intellectual property (IP) to business or creating spin-outs. However, the range of research, knowledge and expertise in universities has wider economic relevance and application beyond technology transfer – the many different forms of unlocking this value are now all referred to as **knowledge exchange (KE)**. They include:

- collaborative and contract research

- consultancy

- access to specialist equipment in universities and colleges

- IP

- the development of professional capabilities to use knowledge (CPD).

Working in partnership with business

Universities seek to serve society for the public good – including helping stimulate economic growth and local development – and this is reflected in their commitment to knowledge exchange as part of their core mission. But universities also gain benefit from KE for their other core activities of research and teaching. Knowledge exchange, for example, may help universities with live projects or internships for students, making their graduates more employable. KE may also provide insights or resources for new research avenues. Universities are particularly interested then in long-term, sustainable partnerships with businesses where there may be a range of opportunities for mutual benefit.

HEFCE's support for knowledge exchange

HEFCE was a leader in defining the policy for HE knowledge exchange and started providing funding to universities for KE in 1999. With support from the government, this funding has continued and grown: university funding for knowledge exchange (HEIF) stands at £150m per annum for the next four years (2011–15). Around 100 universities in England receive this funding and they have considerable flexibility to use funds as they think best to meet the needs of their business and other partners.

An evaluation of HEIF in 2009 demonstrated that for every £1 of HEIF, universities generated on average between £4.90 and £7.10 in income from offering services to the economy and society.

What can universities offer businesses?

HEFCE funding through HEIF provides an infrastructure for knowledge exchange in universities. This includes dedicated access/information points into the university for business inquirers, as well as dedicated knowledge exchange professionals who understand business needs, recognising that businesses, especially SMEs, have considerable pressures on their time and hence need very targeted solutions. KE staff could advise whether the university has relevant knowledge or expertise to solve a business problem or whether the business may need expertise from another university, as research expertise can also be very specialised.

HEIF also supports development of university academics – who will act as the researchers, consultants or developers in KE activity – so that they have skills to work with and understand businesses.

Part of the responsibility of KE professionals employed in universities through HEIF will be to seek out sources of KE funding that may support collaborative projects with business, including venture capital, proof of concept funding or support for technology commercialisation. KE professional staff may then also be able to advise the businesses that they collaborate with on sources of funding for projects and activities of mutual interest.

Focus on SMEs

While all businesses may benefit from university knowledge exchange, SMEs may find it particularly difficult to access this as they may have less capacity and time to link with universities compared with big companies. HEFCE recognises this in the way it funds universities who work with SMEs through HEIF. HEIF is allocated to universities on the basis of a formula related to income from users for all forms of KE activity (businesses, public and third sectors). HEFCE double-weights income from SMEs in the HEIF formula, so the higher costs for universities which work with SMEs are recognised. This helps universities to have in place professional capabilities to understand and respond to the particular problems of SMEs. Universities have a culture of openness, and often help SMEs particularly with business-focused networking, connecting them with other SMEs and with larger businesses, experts, funders, etc.

The future for knowledge exchange

Links between universities and businesses have grown and strengthened in the last few years. In 2003, Richard Lambert, then head of the CBI, carried out a review for the government and noted that less than 20% of businesses had links with HE institutions. The *CBI Education and Skills Survey for 2010* found that 66% of businesses had links with HE institutions. The coalition government has acknowledged considerable progress made in HE-business links in agreeing to continue to fund HEIF in a tougher financial climate, committing a stable level of funding up until 2015. There is continuing and increased expectation from the government that universities will help rapidly with the economic recovery and economic growth of this nation through working closely with businesses.

HEFCE recognises the strategic importance of HEIF and knowledge exchange and its long-term objective is for knowledge exchange activity to be firmly embedded in universities' missions, along with excellence in teaching and research. It will work to ensure that HEIF delivers value for money, and that HE plays a full part in supporting economic recovery and growth as well as the many wider contributions it makes to serve societal interest.

Alice Frost, head of business and community policy, Higher Education Funding Council for England (HEFCE)

Organisation profile

The Higher Education Funding Council for England (HEFCE)

HEFCE promotes and funds high-quality, cost-effective teaching, research and knowledge exchange to meet the diverse needs of students, the economy and society. Its responsibilities are to develop policies, distribute funds, safeguard quality and assure the proper stewardship of public money. It works closely with universities, colleges and other partners to achieve excellence and impact in education and research, and to provide opportunities for all those who have the ability to benefit from higher education. For the academic year 2011–12, HEFCE will distribute £6.5bn of public money to 130 universities and higher education colleges, and 124 directly funded further education colleges.

Higher education's contribution to economy and society

HEFCE is committed to enhancing the contribution HE makes to the economy and society. Universities and colleges already engage with the wider world in many different ways. HEFCE provides specific funds and support that encourage them to do this more effectively and to contribute to economic growth and social development through innovation, enterprise and skills. In return, it seeks to bring the inspiration of that wider world back into universities and colleges.

There are two key strands within HEFCE's work on economy and society.

1. **HEIF**: designed to support and develop a broad range of knowledge exchange activities between universities and colleges and the wider world, which result in economic and social benefit to the UK.

The government has committed funding of £150m per year for the period 2011–15, with high priority given to activity that can help the country's economic growth.

2. **HEFCE's workforce development programme**: working to develop a new relationship between HE and employers. The programme turns on two related goals.

   - The design and delivery of HE courses in partnership with employers.

   - To increase the number of learners in the workplace supported by their employers.

HEFCE will have provided £150m of government funding between 2008–12 to support the workforce development programme. (See p. 98 for further details.)

STAFFORDSHIRE
UNIVERSITY

Making an impact through innovation

Across the West Midlands, Staffordshire University is helping drive economic regeneration.

During the depths of recession, our 'Futures Programme' delivered highly focused knowledge-intensive aid to help strengthen business resilience and retain talent locally.

Via fresh thinking, ground-breaking research and world-class expertise, we continue to invest in our region's economy.

Our Applied Research Centres and Knowledge Transfer Partnerships are assisting organisations across all sectors.

Our considerable expertise in renewable energy is helping businesses to benefit from the transition to low carbon technologies.

From medical devices and patient monitoring technologies to biometric solutions for the fast-moving computer games sector, the projects we co-develop are inspirational and varied.

With three Lord Stafford Awards for innovation, won over the last three years, we are well known for our novel approach.

To discover the innovation and expertise we can bring to your ideas, call: 01782 294178 or email: forbusiness@staffs.ac.uk
www.staffs.ac.uk/forbusiness

■ CREATE THE **DIFFERENCE**

3

Magnets for enterprise

Economically and culturally, universities are making enterprise one of the pillars on which they rest

Do institutions change their character as a result of necessity or inspiration? In the case of today's universities it appears to be both. Economically, they are under an imperative to adapt. Culturally, they have already accepted that enterprise is the form in which they are going to respond.

The financial model on which they operate is being rewritten. Funding from the government is due to fall by £200m a year and the ceiling for tuition fees is rising from £3,000 to £9,000. Such reforms are designed to stimulate competition and improve access, but will raise some fundamental questions for universities about how best to attract students and meet their expectations.

The commercial pressure under which they find themselves operating is likely to be acute, says Joanna Knight, director at Berkshire Consultancy, who produced a report on the big questions for universities, *Degrees of Change*:

"Business as usual is no longer an option. It has become critical for universities to become even more commercially astute if they want to survive in this changing and highly competitive marketplace."

It is possible that some universities might even close, unless they adapt, although the case for becoming more commercial is clearly understood. As Professor Eric Thomas, president of Universities UK said at its annual conference in September 2011:

"A single university is not just the sum of education, research and enterprise as three separate activities. They are all inextricably integrated; each activity is inseparable from the other."

It is a revealing statement of the central role that enterprise is now playing in shaping the future of universities. Dr Carol David Daniel, head of technology transfer at City University, London argues:

"With government subsidies diminishing, universities will need to become more entrepreneurial and will need to explore alternative sources of income.
*   They will have to accept more risks when deciding how to allocate resources and may need to develop new models in support of projects that involve SMEs. Universities will have to think strategically to generate future opportunities. Those that can transform their culture and view of the world will emerge successful."*

There are already clear signs of the transformative power that enterprise is starting to exercise within universities. Among them are the following.

- More and more graduates are opting to become entrepreneurs.
- The universities are creating more support services for new ventures internally and externally.
- More creative ways of engaging with business are being explored.

Taken together, these changes create the potential for universities to become magnets for enterprise, based on a virtuous circle of knowledge, talent and business support.

Start-ups and spin-offs

University start-ups and spin-offs have been on a steadily rising trajectory since 2003. Last year, 2,695 new ventures were created, a rise of 15% on the previous year (*Higher Education Business and Community Interaction Survey*, HEFCE).

Within these figures, a number were directly associated with the university. The majority, however, were independent start-ups by graduates, more and more of whom are opting to become entrepreneurs when they leave. Last year, they created 2,357 new ventures, nearly 90% of the total.

Some of these are based on the projects undertaken during their degrees. James Barham's device for automatically turning off water when it overflows, the Nova-Flo, was developed as part of his studies at London South Bank University. After he graduated, the idea was then developed under the auspices of the university until it was ready for its first round of funding. It is now on sale in the UK, US and other markets around the world.

Other ventures are based on insights into gaps in the market. Fresh Element in Newcastle, for instance, was originally based on an idea to improve the cooking habits of students. By the time they left university, the founders had built up a broader understanding of the food business and now own three restaurants in the city.

All told, such activities are becoming economically significant. In the latest figures, a total of 6,690 university start-ups and spin-offs were employing 28,000 people and turning over £2bn.

Beyond these direct crossovers from the university to the market, there are less tangible, but still significant forms of new business creation. In particular, a new breed of academic entrepreneurs is emerging in high-tech clusters such as Cambridge, who operate within the university and on their own account in getting ideas off the ground.

The support system

Students have been having bright ideas since Isaac Newton was at Cambridge, of course. The difference now is that any prejudice against commerce has long since disappeared. Today, universities see themselves as active agents in encouraging spin-offs and are building up services to support enterprise, both inside and outside the university.

In the West Midlands, for instance, the three Birmingham universities (Aston, Birmingham City and Birmingham) recently ran a programme to encourage graduate enterprise as a way of upping innovation and retaining skills in the region. Over 17 months, support was given to 350 students and at least 30 new businesses have been created so far.

At Innospace, an old mill converted by Manchester Metropolitan University, graduate start-ups are given a number of options for low-cost space and can draw on a wide range of business advice.

Such support is being opened up more generally. At Wolverhampton Business Solutions Centre in the science park at the university, companies from across the region who are interested in growing can draw on expertise and help from the university and its local partners in economic development.

Professor Ian Oakes, vice chancellor for research and enterprise at Wolverhampton, believes the university can be pivotal in helping enterprises create a competitive advantage and then keep shifting the technology frontier as their rivals catch up. He says:

> "Knowledge and skills transfer is now regarded as being strategically important to regional economies. Universities have a role to play in fostering economic growth, establishing new companies, applying new technologies and increasing the skills of the workforce."

It is an argument that has gained wide acceptance in the government's redesign of the structure for business support. In the 18 local economic partnerships (LEP), which have so far been accepted, each one involves institutions from higher or further education. In the LEP for East Sussex, Kent and Essex, for instance, three universities are participating, giving the kind of support to local business envisaged by Professor Oakes.

Experimental terms

To make good on their promise to put enterprise at the centre of their strategies, universities are starting to experiment with the terms on which they engage business.

- Three research universities are bringing intellectual property to the market which would normally languish in the archives because it is too high risk for anyone to invest in it. By taking the radical step of making it available for free on a simple set of terms, Glasgow, King's College London and Bristol are looking to maximise the use of their knowledge and expertise, as well as opening up new mechanisms for bringing technology to market.

- Other universities, such as City University London, are looking at more creative ways of making research projects happen. They will line up grants, for instance, in return for agreeing to award them any resulting contracts. Or they will even look at undertaking on the basis of sharing any future revenue.

- Others such as Derby and Wolverhampton are breaking up the traditional academic schedules to create bite-sized chunks of learning at a time to suit participants, which can then build up into a portfolio of learning over time.

- As well as encouraging academics to consider how their research will translate into the real world, many universities are bringing in business at the inception of a project to comment on how they might eventually adopt it, so balancing "technology push" with "market pull".

- To prevent research seeming too abstract or theoretical, particularly for smaller companies, a number of universities are creating "visualisation" centres to give a hands-on feel for the impact technology and knowledge can have on everyday applications.

Such examples are by no means isolated. Universities across the board are driving towards the market, turning themselves into a hub for finding new value and inspiring the next generation of high-growth ventures.

Manchester
Metropolitan
University

Manchester Metropolitan is *the* University for your business to engage with.

Our Research and Enterprise Services team consists of a network of experienced sector-specific business professionals who talk your language. We offer bespoke business solutions and services tailored to meet your needs; whatever the size of your company or organisation.

To find out why we're working with Tesco, Goldman Sachs, Rolls-Royce, IBM and hundreds of SMEs, just give us a call.

For an informal and friendly chat about what we can do for you call Andy Chance-Hill on **0161 247 1032** or email **a.chance-hill@mmu.ac.uk**

For more information on products and services go to our website: **www.mmu.ac.uk/business**

How innovation is changing

To reach the market, most ideas are now developed in partnership and across disciplines

At universities and in business, the old linear model for developing products is passing. Because knowledge is so open and competition so intense, no-one can realistically expect to exercise end-to-end control in generating an idea, before finding a way of taking it to market.

Take your mobile phone. In its original incarnation, it was largely the result of research undertaken by the handset producer. Ingenious, but nothing like as clever as the device on which you can now experience the web as if it was on a large screen.

Even a decade ago, telecoms operators were largely following up ideas themselves. Today, they are running scores of partnerships to make their smartphones work and keep pace with the market's expectations.

It is a complex challenge to download hundreds of megabits a second in a way that is easy for anyone to use. These kinds of innovations now depend on actively pursuing ideas and knowledge wherever they are and acting on them quickly. Even the largest operators can no longer rely on their own resources. Otherwise, they will find themselves becoming too slow and insular.

Open partnerships

The experience in mobile phones is a pattern that is repeating itself throughout the economy. Innovation is now an open market in which ideas are brought together from numerous sources. As a smaller company, you can scale up quickly by buying in ideas from the knowledge base or you can plug yourself into much larger networks of value.

Most innovation is now fragmented, depending on pulling together a bundle of rights from different disciplines. For these partnerships to work, it has to be clear who owns the IP, how the rewards are going to be shared and who has the right to follow up any ideas that are created. When the economy recovers, it looks likely that the winners are going to be those who learn how to source ideas by bringing different kinds of partnerships together.

As a discipline, innovation is moving in several new directions. All are united by the logic of the value that open partnerships can unlock.

Demand-led research

The views that your customers hold about what you could and should be doing are now more freely and widely expressed than ever. Their insights and complaints can become a powerful source of innovation in its own right.

Producers of computer games, for instance, have written their next edition based on online comments from their most enthusiastic users. Similarly, the boom in ready-to-drink cocktail mixes was not based on any original in-house thinking by the spirits companies. They just noticed from comments online how clubbers liked to give their drinks an extra twist, so creating a completely new category in the market.

In fact, many brands now organise themselves around these changes in consumer behaviour. After spotting a gap and writing a spec, many will sub-contract their research to a university.

Design thinking

To change the game, many enterprises are turning to "design thinking". They realise that they cannot rely on making incremental improvements. Someone will always be faster and cheaper.

Instead, they are thinking like designers to harness creativity and develop transformative ideas. As an approach, it is moving well beyond design's origins in aesthetics to cover a whole range of messy, awkward questions.

So why has it burst out of the studio and into the mainstream? Graham Grant, principal designer at the centre for design and innovation (C4Di) at Robert Gordon University says:

> *"Designers have the ability to think, not 'what is?', but 'what could be?' They are able to envisage multiple solutions to problems, visualise them, create stories about them and prototype them. Designers have learnt to identify problems and contradictions, to create insights from human behaviours, and to design elegant solutions to unmet needs."*

First, you gather insights into how users are behaving and the irritations they are experiencing, which you record in as many forms as you can, both written and visual. You want to gain a proper understanding of the real problem that is being faced.

Only then do you start to generate ideas by thinking as divergently as possible, imagining as many as solutions as you can, none of which you dismiss as too wild or unlikely. The emphasis is on cross-disciplinary teamwork on the grounds that few ideas ever emerge fully formed from a single source. By encouraging multiple inputs from across the organisation, you bridge different fields of knowledge, encourage buy-in and unify your approach to innovation.

Once you have a full palette of ideas, you can filter them down and select the most promising ones to develop into prototypes. These are early-stage models made from cardboard, sticky tape, Plasticine or Lego. It gives you a concrete form, however rough, to gauge reaction from the people who will actually use them, says Grant, who helps enterprises to re-design their futures at C4Di, using tools for creative visualisation to produce insights into how we behave.

Based on what everyone thinks, you can then develop more sophisticated concepts. If you have run it as an interdisciplinary project, involving directors, accountants and marketing, it is unlikely to be killed off at this stage. Even if it does fail, says Grant, you will learn from the experience within the innovative culture that design thinking creates.

Meeting of minds: Knowledge Transfer Networks

At the limits of what you know, you often make the most unexpected and rewarding connections. It's when an idea crosses from one setting to another that the most lucrative sources of business advantage are found.

As an innovator, it pays to explore disciplines just beyond your reach. If you specialise in fuel cells for cars, then talk to someone who is making batteries for PCs. Similarly, if you are designing low-carbon buildings, you might ask a psychologist about how home-buyers will feel about your new materials.

Although unexpected, such connections are often the point when real innovation begins. But how do you find them? You could leave it to chance. Or you could join one of the networks for different forms of knowledge run by bodies like the Technology Strategy Board.

Its Knowledge Transfer Networks (KTNs) are designed to engineer a meeting of minds between business and research. Within a national framework, you will find 15 specialist groups which are designed to let you find the right person with the right knowledge at the right time.

On its web platform (www.innovateuk.org/deliveringinnovation/ knowledgetransfernetworks.ashx), you can explore potential crossovers using a free set of online tools. By joining a community, you can also keep up to date with news about funding and research.

The networks cover the following disciplines:

- aerospace, aviation and defence
- biosciences
- chemistry
- creative industries
- electronics, sensors, photonics
- energy generation and supply
- environmental sustainability
- financial services
- health tech and medicines
- information and communications technology
- industrial mathematics
- materials
- modern built environment
- nanotechnology
- transport.

Challenge-led innovation

As well as business, governments are actively looking for innovative solutions in the challenges they face. An ageing population. Zero-carbon buildings. Intelligent transport systems. Sustainable agriculture. Detection of new infections. Only so much can be achieved through new legislation or by launching grand projects.

Since 2008, the Technology Strategy Board in the UK has been creating a process for combining social, commercial and economic perspectives to pull innovation through from frontline research. The result is a series of innovation platforms which bring together policy-makers, academics, business leaders and entrepreneurs to map out how these markets might develop in future.

From the questions they identify, competitions and demonstrations are spun out to find solutions or break logjams. SMEs are actively encouraged to bid for this work through the Small Business Research Initiative (SBRI).

Process innovation

As well as outcomes in the forms of new products and services, innovation is as much about new working processes, encouraging all parts of an organisation to challenge the norms and assumptions on which you operate.

- How are your customers' expectations changing?
- Can you find ways to work smarter?
- Is your business model out of date?
- How can you use digital technologies to turn yourself into a "network company" and eliminate costs?

Such open innovation is about the flows of knowledge in and out of the organisation, says Peter Ives at Business Dynamix. He says:

> "It sounds a complex process but actually only involves establishing networks of players who can add value to each other. Universities and other higher educational institutes are key factors in providing access to leading thinking in most areas of business operation."

Lean business models

Science and engineering remain at the core of innovation. By making a technical breakthrough or developing a master idea, you can open up a market in which everyone has to buy from you.

Since the financial crash of 2008, however, the model for getting such innovations off the ground has changed. Few investors are willing to support a venture all the way through the early stages. Money is too tight for complex science and complex technology.

Others are thinking differently. In their search for the next blockbuster, major players in areas such as the life sciences accept the logic of open innovation. You may be surprised by how willing they are to talk to you. Instead of asking for money upfront to prove your concept, you have to be prepared to construct a lean business model and trade your IP.

As well as your share of future revenues, you might be able to ask for some funding against project milestones. Or you could act as a consultant. Further funding could come from public research programmes or medical charities. In these early stages, you can keep yourself lean and tight, as you conduct the first round of tests and collect the data to give your IP credibility in the market.

PART 2
The transfer market

5

Commercial capability

Universities are now a professional service to bring knowledge into the market

In the last 10 years, universities have transformed their commercial capabilities. Up until then, as an SME, you would have found yourself tracking down a lone industrial liaison officer, who was charged with looking after a thousand academics and a thousand researchers. No surprise that it was difficult to find your way around.

Universities such as Strathclyde and Imperial had started to pioneer a more commercial approach in the late 80s and early 90s, actively looking at ways to take their research and expertise to market. By the early 2000s, spurred by the belief that universities were the cogs on which the knowledge economy was going to turn and a major policy push, nearly all of them had established a "technology transfer office". The idea was to draw on the rigour and discipline of academics in developing ready-for-market innovations.

Many of these offices are now evolving into knowledge transfer offices or even knowledge exchanges on the following grounds.

- **Knowledge is a two-way multi-dimensional flow between a university and its business partners.**

- Innovation is moving beyond its technical core in science and engineering, embracing softer forms of know-how and including disciplines such as the social sciences and humanities.

Where the old industrial liaison officer would occupy a solitary post, the knowledge exchange has typically grown into teams of 20–30 people. In the case of research powerhouses, such as Oxford or Imperial, the headcount is closer to 70 and specialist technology accelerators have been spun out as standalone companies. Other knowledge exchanges have deliberately kept themselves within the university to keep close to the academics who are conducting the research.

In whatever form they take, these offices are designed to act as translators to frame your query in the right way. Often, for instance, companies expect to commission some research, when in fact it is just a matter of an expert mapping out the territory and producing some options.

As well as expanding the boundaries of knowledge, a university is educating the next generation of talent and its careers office will have created its own set of tools for bringing students and graduates into your company. Again, size is no barrier. You will find that most universities are hungry to grow their transfer activities and are ready to find ways of collaborating with SMEs. You simply have to be clear on your objectives.

Alongside these services, a knowledge transfer office is looking to bring the university's own technology and know-how to market in the following ways.

- It encourages and supports start-ups from graduates and students.
- It spins out research into new ventures.
- It licenses its knowledge to business partners who can bring it to market.
- It sets up collaborations to run research programmes.

To make all these activities happen, it will often act as a gateway to finance, both for grants from official bodies in the UK and the EU, and as a filter for early-stage capital from private investors.

Innovation capacity

The growth in knowledge exchange is underpinned by government policy and funding. Each year, in excess of £150m goes into building up the commercial capabilities of Britain's universities. Even following the cuts, this funding has been guaranteed through to 2015.

The much larger amounts of public money that are spent on funding research are also being tied more closely to social and economic impacts. From 2014, under the Research Excellence Framework, this element will account for 20% of the core research funding of any university (known as "QR": quality-related) alongside more traditional academic criteria.

Nationally, such policies are having an effect.

- Seven hundred spin-outs have been created in the last seven years.
- Over 70 of these have gone to flotation or trade sale at a total valuation of £9bn.
- The universities are earning £56m a year from their intellectual property.
- Income from contract research stands at £950m and from collaborative research at £750m.

On the basis of these figures, many observers accept that the UK is now close to reaching the same level of performance as the US. In Europe, the UK is generally recognised as leading the way in knowledge transfer among universities, although countries such as Germany are stronger in other areas, such as its technology and innovation centres, the Fraunhofer.

University returns

At a national level, the benefits for the UK in bringing research closer to the market are clear. Originally, many universities expected to see the same kind of steady financial returns. In reality, they are more likely to break even year on year.

The difficulty lies in commercialising complex ideas and technologies and the need for those taking major financial risks to secure a return. First you have to screen a hundred candidates, then invest in developing 10, only one of which might ever make it to market. From any proceeds, you have to meet the cost of funding the other nine.

For universities, these commercial activities are recognised as having wider benefits. In bringing ideas from the lab into the real world, you make yourself more relevant and appealing to students, and you open up new, relevant lines of inquiry.

Taking a longer view over the 10 years that it takes to investigate a complex technology, there is the scope for a major one-off return on sale or flotation. Typically, any proceeds are split three ways: a third to the university to invest back into its core activities; a third to the school or faculty where the idea originated; and a third to the academics to encourage them and their colleagues to keep finding ways of commercialising their knowledge.

Expert comment by Professor Dave Delpy, Research Councils UK Impact Champion

Bringing research and business together

In the late 1990s, when Professor Shankar Balasubramanian and his colleague David Klenerman, bumped into each other in the Cambridge University tea room little did they know that years later their research partnership would develop the world's leading DNA sequencing product and that their spin-out company, Solexa, would be sold for $600m making it the most successful the university had ever seen. Funded by the Biotechnology and Biological Sciences Research Council (BBSRC), Professor Balasubramanian was named Innovator of the Year in 2010 and the success of Solexa shows that working in partnership can create excellent business opportunities that have an impact on wider society in the UK and around the world.

Research Councils UK (RCUK) has developed successful collaborations between business and UK universities to ensure long-term partnerships are forged. Such partnerships have a positive impact on the economic and social wellbeing of the UK, maximise the impact of investment in research and generate highly skilled graduates needed by business. RCUK is responsible for investing around £3bn a year into research in UK universities. The seven Research Councils that make up the RCUK partnership cover the full spectrum of academic disciplines from the medical and biological sciences to astronomy, physics, chemistry, mathematics and engineering, social sciences, economics, environmental sciences and the arts and humanities.

Between them the Research Councils support various schemes and initiatives to ensure the researchers they fund have the opportunity to work in collaboration with non-academic partners. All the Research Councils have close links with businesses which have been developed over a number of years. As these relationships have become more productive, RCUK has been considering how to maximise their impact. The Engineering and Physical Sciences Research Council (EPSRC), for example, has invested in 12 new national EPSRC Centres for Innovative Manufacturing based at universities across the UK. These Centres will undertake cutting-edge research to address major long-term manufacturing challenges and/or emergent market opportunities, and will enhance the global profile and significance of UK manufacturing research. Each EPSRC Centre is supported by leading industry partners and a range of high-tech small and medium-sized enterprises across a whole range of sectors.

A similar initiative has recently been launched by the Arts and Humanities Research Council (AHRC). The new AHRC Knowledge Exchange Hubs for the creative economy provide a unique opportunity for universities to work in partnership with creative businesses and cultural organisations. Overall there is a high level of varied interactions between academics in the arts and humanities and business, ranging from participating in networks, to providing informal advice and consultancy services. These new Hubs will help increase the number of arts and humanities researchers working in collaboration with the creative industries.

It is well known that UK universities attract the very best academics and students from around the world, as well as investment from multinational, research intensive businesses. The Research Councils close partnerships with universities allow them to spot, develop and promote research excellence to keep the UK at the top of the world standings and find innovative solutions to global challenges. To support their researchers, all of the Research Councils offer Collaborative Awards in Science and Engineering (CASE) studentships which involve PhD research being carried out in collaboration with a business partner. The Medical Research Council (MRC), for example, provides a number of Industrial CASE opportunities. One recipient of the award is Emily Davies, a PhD student at the University of Bristol, who said of the experience: "I was keen to get experience of industry as well as academic research during my PhD, so the CASE award was perfect for me. It involved a commitment of three months with GlaxoSmithKline (GSK) in addition to the standard three years at the University of Bristol. In the end, I was at GSK's Clinical Unit in Cambridge for eight months so that I could see my research project through from start to finish. I am still in touch with the team there, helping write up a paper and maintaining the collaboration."

Schemes such as those mentioned above give small to medium-sized organisations access to cutting-edge research they might be unable to conduct themselves. Large multinational organisations often conduct their research and development in-house, but even these companies seek out expertise within UK universities. Knowledge exchange between researchers and business can have benefits for both parties and helps ensure cutting-edge research can contribute to UK business growth. The Natural Environment Research Council (NERC) has a number of knowledge exchange and commercialisation schemes in place and is very keen to encourage researchers to link up with industry. It has dedicated commercialisation managers working within its own research centres, with higher education institutes and with industries, who sniff out potential research-to-business ideas that will meet current and future market demands.

The most successful commercialisation of NERC research comes in the form of MTEM Ltd. The company arose from a NERC funded PhD at Edinburgh University and is Scotland's largest academic spin-out. MTEM developed pioneering electromagnetic survey technology which has the potential to provide oil companies with huge savings by determining whether reservoirs contain oil and gas before they incur drilling costs. It was sold for $275m in June 2007 to Petroleum Geo-Services.

As well as adding value to the UK economy, the value of research to business has been demonstrated many times over when you consider the number of successful innovations, scientific discoveries, spin-out companies and collaborations. RCUK directly engages with around 2,500 companies, with 21% of PhD projects having formal collaboration arrangements with business and industry partners. To encourage researchers to think more about the commercial applications of their work the Science and Technology Facilities Council (STFC) offers support to researchers who want to turn their research into a viable business. STFC Innovations Ltd identifies and brokers deals with business and industry to help commercialise research. It currently has a portfolio of 59 patent families of which half are already licensed. The majority of these have potential for licensing or as the basis for a spin-out company.

Almost all Research Councils work with researchers to inspire their entrepreneurial side. For the last 15 years, the Biotechnology and Biological Sciences Research Council (BBSRC) has run the Biotechnology Young Entrepreneurs Scheme (YES), a competition to raise awareness of the commercialisation of bioscience ideas among postgraduate students and postdoctoral scientists. An investigation into the career paths followed by researchers who participated in YES between 1996–2002 showed that a larger proportion went on to work in the private sector than other BBSRC funded students. One such student was Tim Hart. Tim competed in Biotechnology YES in 1997 as managing director of a team from the University of Surrey and has since supported Biotechnology YES as a mentor, presenter and judge. Tim is now CEO of Zyoxel, a spin-out company which has secured £1m investment from Hong Kong multinational CN Innovations Holdings to develop microbioreactors.

This demonstrates that the impact of research is felt outside of universities. The talented people conducting this research are assets to the business community. The Economic and Social Research Council (ESRC) supports business by establishing partnerships with social scientists. One such partnership, funded by ESRC through the Knowledge Transfer Partnerships (KTP) scheme, between researchers at Surrey University and BT explored human patterns of communication across written, spoken and electronic media. The project gave BT new insights into the ways in which people use different communications mechanisms as part of their daily lives and has already led to a number of new product ideas.

RCUK also invests in and provides access to world-class research facilities. For example, the Daresbury and Harwell Science and Innovation Campuses provide a unique environment for innovation and business growth. Each campus is a vibrant and growing community of science and technology-based innovation and enterprise. Over 4,500 people now work on the Harwell Campus in some 100 organisations.

To fully support UK business and industry, a continuing supply of excellent researchers and highly skilled people generated by our universities is needed. RCUK is responsible for the single largest investment in researchers in UK higher education and actively encourages and enables the movement of researchers between academic institutions and business and industry, at all career stages.

Professor Dave Delpy, Research Councils UK Impact Champion. For more information about Research Councils UK, visit www.rcuk.ac.uk.

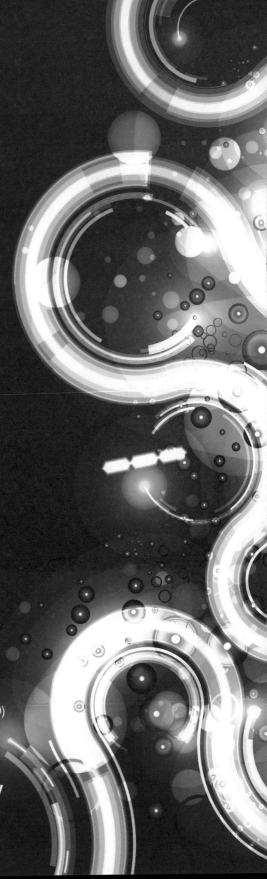

6

Approaching a university

How to navigate your way around higher education and find the right people

As an SME, you can draw on knowledge in a university to fix a problem, pull in an expert, explore a new line of business, test an idea or open up a market. Who exactly do you ask though? And what do you tell them?

It can be harder than you think, says Douglas Robertson, Director of Research and Enterprise Services at Newcastle University and this year's chairman of Praxis Unico, the specialist body in knowledge transfer.

The real question

Essentially, you have two approaches, depending on how fully you appreciate the nature of the challenge you are facing.

If you have a clear spec, then you can probably track down the kind of expert you need through a university's online directory. Alternatively talk to your trade association or chamber of commerce. Or work through one of the Knowledge Transfer Networks (KTN) run by the Technology Strategy Board.

Then send them a summary of how you would like them to help, says Robertson:

> *"If you express yourself clearly, we can tell you straightaway what we can do. Often SMEs think we will have to conduct some research. In fact, they usually need a consultant to lay out all their technical options. Research is only for when no-one has ever looked at something before."*

When it works, this approach is fast and efficient. Most universities have a central email address with recipients ready to turn round these kinds of inquiry. The one at Newcastle, for instance, is business@nct.ac.uk.

But many emails are hard to fathom, Robertson finds:

> *"Databases of expertise are great if you know exactly what you are looking for. Most SMEs don't. In the thick of running a business, it can be hard to see the wider picture and figure out the real question.*
>
> *Inevitably, you are bounded by your own experience. It helps to have an intelligent interface. So my advice is to pick up the phone. A five-minute call is always more productive than a long, intricate email."*

However, the real skill is what Robertson calls "knowledge elicitation". He adds: "As an enterprise, you rarely, if ever, talk to a university. We are in touch with them the whole time and have spent 10 years learning how to find the right focus."

Your expectations

In approaching a university, it helps to understand what it actually offers. You might like to think it is an agency within the government's infrastructure for business support. In fact, universities are autonomous charitable institutions whose primary role is research and education. So for basic advice on how to run your business, you should probably start at your chamber of commerce.

For queries on accessing talent, just about any SME could contact a university. On technical questions, the university will gravitate towards anyone who is creating new ideas or testing the boundaries. For academics to take time away from their core activities of research and teaching, it has to be a project that engages their interest. Otherwise, you might be better talking to a business consultant, says Robertson.

Better questions quicker

There is no standard format for organising a knowledge transfer office. Each university has evolved in its own distinctive way. However, many are now putting in a place a structure that cuts out any layers and allows you to talk directly to each centre of expertise.

At Newcastle, for instance, each of the three main faculties has its knowledge transfer team, who know the particular characteristics of their academics and where their research is heading. In the life sciences, you tend to be at the pure end of the scientific spectrum. In engineering, you are closer to market. "Our aim," says Robertson, "is to be as responsive as we can in answering the challenges that enterprises face."

Support schemes

In England, many of the support schemes that regional development agencies ran to support such interactions between university and enterprise have disappeared. So discussions have had to become more directly commercial.

In Scotland, Wales and Northern Ireland, many of these schemes still exist in forms such as innovation vouchers, which give grants in the region of £5,000 to let SMEs undertake an initial assignment with a university.

Throughout the UK, Knowledge Transfer Partnerships remain the flagship programme for facilitating the placement of graduates within companies for between one and three years. Two-thirds of the cost is met through a grant in recognition of the value that is created for the university in undertaking these kinds of collaborative project. As an SME, you pay for the rest. It has proved an effective and popular scheme for finding new solutions and making improvements.

For other SMEs, many universities in England, including Newcastle and Aston, have run their own independent version of innovation vouchers. It is designed to let SMEs try working with a university by undertaking an assignment worth up to £5,000 at no cost.

"As universities, we want to encourage SMEs to build a relationship with us and undertake future engagements," says Robertson. "Here, 125 new business relationships emerged over a six-month period."

As an SME, your first challenge is to ask the right questions of the right people. Once you have a firm foundation, a powerful two-way process of knowledge transfer can then start to develop.

Dr Douglas Robertson is Director of Research & Enterprise Services, Newcastle University and Chair of PraxisUnico, the UK's leading organisation for research commercialisation professionals. Douglas graduated with First Class Honours from Aberdeen University, followed by a PhD from the University of Wales in the early 1980s. A research administration post at the University of Leeds then led to management positions at Strathclyde, Nottingham and now Newcastle. He has a passion for seeing the fruits of research into application. His brief at Newcastle covers external research funding (£220m book value), research strategy and policy, patents, licensing, spin-out companies, support for international partnerships and economic impact of the University in the region. A quasi-public sector career has been interspersed at various times with directorships of many young technology businesses, including nine years as a director for a Midlands-based civil engineering consultancy employing more than 80 people. Board memberships include NES General Partner Ltd (overseeing management of an investment fund); Alcyomics Ltd (a university spin-out company); ASTEC Ltd; Codeworks Ltd (an ICT industrial network); PraxisUnico (the UK research commercialisation association); NUIB pte Ltd (Singapore); Clarizon Ltd (a university spin-out); and NUIS pte Ltd. For further details see: www.praxisunico.org.uk.

7

How academic and commercial priorities differ

Understanding the expectations of each party to build a productive relationship

Universities are proving their worth in furthering the knowledge and testing the assumptions on which enterprises are built. But they can be unusual partners. Their view is different from the everyday commercial world. They certainly operate at a different pace and some would say they speak a different language. If you are going to work with them, it pays to know where they are coming from.

Essentially, they are charities whose primary role is to educate their students and expand the field of knowledge. Over the last 20 years, they have become more commercially engaged. In part, they are looking to raise funds, but they are also aiming to benefit us all socially, environmentally and economically. The profits they make in working with business go back into building up their core activities in the creation and communication of knowledge.

As a bridge to the market, their knowledge transfer offices have developed a set of tools for businesses to access expertise, talent and research. Yet the decision on the degree to which knowledge is going to be put to commercial use rests with the academics themselves.

As researchers and educators, they have a different agenda from businesses. Yes, they are encouraged to become more connected to business by the funders of their research and educational activities. Yes, they have a chance to make a return from their share of any IP that reaches the market. But they have other, equally strong motives.

- Their careers often depend on pursuing interesting new lines of inquiry.
- They want to prove their own credentials by publishing research and appearing at conventions.
- They want the graduates under their charge to complete their theses.
- They want their students to see they are connected to the real world.

These are all laudable aims, of course, but they do not always sit easily within a commercial context. You will have the knowledge transfer office to act as a translator, of course, but the value of your engagement with a university is likely to depend in the end on the relationship you forge with the experts in your field.

Initial risks

Many of the primary risks in these relationships have been overcome. True, academics can still over-estimate the value of their IP and how close it is to market. After 20 years of commercial experience, however, there is a sharper understanding of how difficult it is to transfer knowledge and commercialise it.

Similarly, the ambition among academics to head any spin-outs is falling. Both they and their employers at the university see little point in trading in years of academic expertise to have a tilt at running a new venture. Keep them involved. Make them the technical director. But the preference now is usually to leave the commercial decisions to a business manager.

One risk that you are still likely to encounter is a different sense of time. Exams and conferences are what matter in the academic calendar, not your target date for breakeven.

In forming a partnership, you will want to consider putting in place some controls.

- Check the commercial experience of your partners.
- Produce a clear spec of what you are trying to achieve.
- Set a realistic timeline based on the size of your budget and take into account their other research commitments.

- Ask about what grants the university can access to support your programme.

- Keep your lines of communications open through the course of the project: academics have been known to pursue interesting tangents, rather than the question you are asking them.

Moderate expectations

As someone who is building a business, you will expected to be clear cut in your agreements. On three key points, where disputes and complications frequently occur, it will help if you understand where the university is coming from: these areas are confidentiality, intellectual property and guarantees.

1. You want to be as confidential as possible, but the university wants to be free to publish the results and use them for teaching. Be realistic. You cannot tie down the university as a whole. Limit the restrictions to those in the know on the research team. Keep it straightforward. Your academic partners will almost always be happy to ask you before they publish the results. They are not going to be irresponsible, but enterprises always tend to be surprised about how important the freedom to publish is to them.

2. You will expect to retain the rights in any intellectual property. Think again, unless you are sponsoring the whole programme. It is much more common for you to have exclusivity for any direct, commercial results. Any surrounding or extra knowledge rests with the university.

3. Normally, you would ask your supplier to guarantee their results. It is unlikely the university will agree on the grounds that all research is speculative. No-one knows what the answers will be. Instead, ask them to apply the highest professional and ethical standards in their research.

These assumptions will be woven into the university's standard terms. Rather than seeing them as sharp negotiating, as you might in a more straightforward commercial setting, see them as a reflection of the university's overall mission. You will save yourself a lot of time and grief.

The value of trust

There are other powerful reasons for reaching an understanding of where you both stand. Innovation often happens when two opposing views or two separate disciplines collide. There might be friction at these interfaces, but you can suddenly open up new ways of thinking.

You might have a tight brief for the project you have in mind, but academics always appreciate having an open discussion first. Talk through all the possibilities before locking yourself into one line of inquiry or into a set methodology.

Once you have reached a realistic agreement, it pays to keep up a regular dialogue with the university. It can often result in the most creative forms of knowledge transfer.

You might even try thinking like an academic yourself. Contribute to a paper. Give a talk to the students. You might be surprised by how much extra value you can create by stepping into the academic world, even if it is just for a moment.

Seven barriers to collaboration

The EEF, the voice of British manufacturing, in its report entitled *New Light on Innovation* (2006), highlighted seven barriers to collaboration for the purposes of innovation:

- finding the right partner
- understanding your business
- managing costs
- relationship management
- keeping control of ideas
- legal form of the relationship
- intellectual property rights.

8

Intellectual property and the ownership of ideas

How to straighten out the terms for different forms of collaboration

The combination between a university's specialist knowledge and an enterprise's dynamic execution is a powerful source of innovation. By forging connections and partnerships, you can take the lead in your market, rather than trying to catch up.

Yet the potential in such collaborations often falls short because of misunderstandings about who owns the intellectual property in the results and how these commercial rights can best be managed.

The process of turning a raw piece of research into a ready-for-market application is one of the toughest challenges in business. When managed well, a portfolio of intellectual property in the form of patents, trademarks, copyright, designs, domains and know-how can:

- put you ahead of the market
- lock in a commercial advantage

- prevent anyone adopting your approach
- give you the freedom to operate
- let you charge a premium.

One tempting route to secure these benefits is to agree to joint ownership of any intellectual property you create. It might work, but more usually it stores up trouble for later. If you both have a say in how the IP is going to be used, you can easily block yourselves out. One alternative is to spin out a separate company to own, fund and manage the rights, then pay each partner a dividend on any returns.

In most cases, it is best to agree a set of terms for your collaboration in advance. To speed up this process, the Intellectual Property Office has created a series of models and templates, which you can download for free (see Appendix 2).

None of these agreements will capture all the particular features of any one project, but they do give you a basis on which to negotiate, allowing you to focus on the main sticking points. Agreements that once took months to finalise can now be put together in a matter of days.

Model agreements

To get you up to speed, an interactive decision guide clarifies your stance towards three underlying questions that will determine the nature of your relationship. Who is going to own and use the IP? Who is paying for the research? How are the results going to be used for academic purposes?

You will then be directed towards one of five model agreements. The first three models cover initial lines of inquiry in which the university holds the IP and an enterprise gains varying degrees of exclusivity to exploit it. The fourth and fifth models cover deeper collaboration which rely on technical and financial input from the enterprise. The fourth model is widely used: the enterprise gains the IP, but the university has the right to use for it for non-commercial purposes. The fifth model covers contract research, where the university cannot use the results without permission.

In practice, enterprises often approach universities with queries for research, which turn out to be consultancy assignments. No new knowledge is being created and the academic prepares a report on the options that an enterprise has. A template is also available on the IPO's website.

Sticking points

In dealing with a university, it is always best to be clear about who exactly owns the IP on their side. As an employer, the university will normally expect to own the IP that its academics and graduates create in the course of their research. Undergraduates, who are paying for their courses, are generally free to exploit their own ideas. But take care to track down anyone else who might have a claim: is a corporation sponsoring any programmes? Is there a visiting fellow who works at another university? You do not want any surprises later.

As an SME, your collaborations will normally be one-offs, while you continue to run the rest of your business. Naturally, you will be concerned about injecting funds into any existing IP. Similarly, the university will want to retain a right to its own background technology. One answer is to identify any existing IP then license it to each other.

For anything new you create, IP is not a prize, but a set of tools, which has to fit into your commercial strategy. For a platform technology in areas such as life sciences and engineering, you may well be happy to build a business round a patent. In software, where speed to market counts, you might rely on copyright.

If you are sitting on a potential blockbuster, you might be willing to stake everything on one broad claim. The risk of creating a single point of failure is offset by the chance of scaling it up quickly.

It is more likely that you will create a layer of rights. You might register a patent for the part of an innovation which the market really values or which blocks off your competitors, but use other rights such as copyright, designs, confidentiality and trade secrets for everything else. You can still protect your exclusivity, as well as creating more commercial options and keeping your costs down.

IP tends to be a snapshot of an idea at a single point in time. Ideally, you want to make sure that you can continue to access all the knowledge and experience that sits around it. In any case, you want to be clear about who has the rights to follow up any of the results of your research in future. In particular, you would like to know if an academic subsequently unearths a hidden gem.

In the original excitement of creating and launching an innovation, it can be hard to imagine that an agreement could end in dispute. Of course, it happens. To prevent the cost and complication of litigation, it is always worth agreeing in advance an alternative form of resolution, such as arbitration or mediation.

It is better to set up your IP so it does not become a divisive issue. Allyson Reed, director of strategy and communications at the Technology Strategy Board says:

"Before you reach the stage of everyone trying to ring-fence their IP, you have to work out the interests of the various partners. In the best cases, people have different interests at different points in the value chain. You construct win-win partnerships. Yes, you must protect your IP, but you must find different ways of using it and be flexible.

You have to understand the context. It is tough to voice the market need in a way that allows you to be open to a range of different solutions. You have to be realistic about the risks and about how close to market you actually are. Innovation is about much more than the core piece of technology. You have to get all the pieces together. When it works, it really is worth it, because its gives you such a sustainable competitive advantage."

For further details, about the Intellectual Property Office's model agreements for one-to-one collaboration between a business and university, as well as those for consortiums, see www.ipo.gov.uk/lambert. For sample consultancy agreements and confidentiality notices, look under the section titled "useful resources" (www.ipo.gov.uk/whyuse/research/lambert/lambert-resources.htm).

Profit from
knowledge

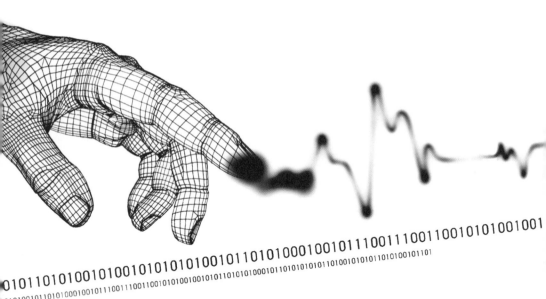

Excellence in innovation, accessible to your business

To find out how we can help your business, contact the Office of Innovation:

www.ulster.ac.uk/innovation

Office of Innovation | T: +44 (0) 28 9036 8019 | enquiry@ulster.ac.uk

Courses | Research | Working with Business and the Community

Department for
**Employment
and Learning**
www.delni.gov.uk

9

How to look for innovation

Identifying the technologies and ideas that can support innovation

Everyone recognises the need for businesses of all sizes and in all sectors to innovate in order to prosper, especially if you are a technology company. But if you are a small company without the luxury of the resources of multinationals or large corporates, how do you do this effectively and where do you start?

"With more and more web-based tools available, small technology companies as well as large, can now be much more effective at identifying technologies and ideas that can help their businesses be more innovative. All for an investment of an hour or two online," says Mark Thompson, formerly head of market development at the University of Manchester Intellectual Property (UMIP).

Open innovation

Over the last 10 years, open innovation has gained wide acceptance. Ideas and technologies are flowing in and out of major innovators, who have reduced their reliance on internal R&D and are switching resources to a dedicated search for external innovation through activities such as patent mapping, technology scouting, corporate venturing or publicly promoting their "interest" areas. Philips for example, employs 250 people just in its in-licensing, IP management and out-licensing department alone.

"We now have a situation where open innovation, along with the increased recognition of IP protection and improved access to universities, creates a stimulating, dynamic and complex scene," says Thompson, who was named by *Intellectual Asset Management* magazine in 2009 as one of the world's top 250 IP strategists and who is now running his consultancy on open innovation in low carbon.

Despite the attractions, even experienced and well-resourced large corporates frequently complain that the technology world is a frustrating jungle. In a closed model of innovation, you only have to look internally for innovations. But now if you are seeking a solution, it could come from potentially any organisation anywhere, including a choice of 9,000 universities worldwide.

The smaller tech venture

As a smaller technology or manufacturing venture, where do you start looking for innovation? Do you have time to turn yourself into an expert on web resources? Can you work out how to use online patent databases?

However, there are now a wide variety of other online tools and networks or SMEs to use allowing you to:

- find a solution for a specific technical problem
- find innovative technologies that could be translated into a product
- keep track of innovation activities in specific sectors
- monitor competitors.

These resources are described one by one below, forming a box of complementary tools. Not all are completely free, but even on the commercial ones, you can gain some value at no cost.

Google or Yahoo alerts

It is surprising how many people have not heard of these. In essence these allow anyone to set up an email alert notifying them when something new has come onto the web matching specific search terms that you set. You can set up as many different alerts as you wish. So, if you are in the water quality sector, you could have one alert set up for identifying new web content on "innovative water treatment technology" and perhaps another for "Danfoss new product".

Technology portals

Emerging over the last six or seven years, these sites are online databases which are either completely free or have useful free functionality. They either list new licensable technologies, or technologies/innovations being sought, or both. The main portals are compared in the following tables.

Portals that list just technologies available

www.ibridgenetwork.org	Technologies from US universities only. Information in reasonable lay language although quite wordy. No fees or charges for contacting advertisers. Sliding scale of fees to list technology.
www.prior-ip.com	US bias, data almost entirely in patent text format so not easy reading, data can be browsed freely but registration and payment required to see full information and to allow users to contact advertisers. Fees to list technology.
www.flintbox.com	Data from Canadian universities only. Data is in a digestible lay language format. No fees of any kind. Users can contact advertisers freely. Email alerts facility.
http://emarket.knowledgeexpress.com	Data format not very structured and visually not easy on the eye for browsing. Data tends to be in patent language. Free to browse part of data but registration necessary to view full text. Advertisers can only be contacted through Knowledge Express. Expensive to advertise.
www.university-technology.com	Scottish universities only. Good data format. Users can contact advertisers directly. No fees.

Portals that list just technology needs

www.innocentive.com	Technology needs are usually large multinational. Data usually in a good concise data format. Free to browse. Contact advertisers through Innocentive only. Expensive to advertise on. Email alerts.
www.ninesigma.com	Technology needs are usually from large multinationals. Usually good concise data format. Free to browse. Contact advertisers through Ninesigma only. Expensive to advertise on. Email alerts facility.

Portals that list both technologies available and technology needs

www.tynax.com	US bias. Registered users can add their data directly. Free to browse. Data heavy text format. 25% deal fee to anyone advertising a technology request or technology offer. Advertisers can only be contacted indirectly through Tynax. Data format quite heavyweight. Email alerts facility.
www.yet2.com	Centred around US but also covers UK, Japan to a degree. Good lay language data format. Email alerts facility.
www.theintellectualproperty.net (IP Net)	International profile. Very concise data format and very easy to browse. Mainly university IP. No fees. Users directly upload their own technology offers or needs data. Users can contact advertisers directly. Email alerts facility.

The last of these, IP Net, is the newest, being the first portal of this sort to allow anyone, anywhere to advertise a technology offering or an innovation need for free. This and the ability for users to register online and add and control their content directly, make it extremely easy for SMEs in particular to use.

Where sites allow users to register for email alerts or updates for new technologies, key word filters can usually be set. A number also have an RSS feed, which works very well, particularly as the volume of new traffic flowing out of these systems is relatively modest.

Halfbakery

www.halfbakery.com is a free open website for people to directly post their "half-baked" ideas for product or technology innovations for the good of society. It can be quite creative and unusual, although all the ideas (or part ideas) are public domain. If you find an idea, you cannot be sure that someone else is using it as well.

The Knowledge Vine

www.theknowledgevine.net is a free email-based networking system consisting of 1,000 or so technology professionals, from a wide variety of organisations including 200 universities internationally. It allows users to post a "single sentence question" to others by email, so it is ideal for locating technologies for specific purposes, eg "Does anyone know of a technology that ...?" Users reply just to the person asking the question if they know someone that can help.

Knowledge Transfer Networks

www.ktnetworks.co.uk – the KTNs are technology specific networks for the UK, run by the Technology Strategy Board. There are some 19 different ones covering subject areas from fuel cells through to creative industries. They are all free to join, and run events, newsletters etc. They give a very good means of keeping up to speed with trends, issues and opportunities in specific sectors and have a very good entrepreneurial and communal feel. You can join online for free.

List of technology transfer networks

- aerospace, aviation and defence
- biosciences
- chemistry innovation
- creative industries
- electronics, sensors, photonics
- energy generation and supply
- environmental sustainability
- financial services
- healthtech and medicines
- ICT
- industrial mathematics
- materials
- modern built environment
- nanotechnology
- transport

Patent searching

The idea of a patent is to reward innovators and give them a period of exclusivity. In return it is designed to put advances in technology into the public domain. By reading the document you gain an understanding of what an innovation does and how it works.

On free-to-use databases, you can search by your type of technology, by your sector of the market, by the name of a competitor or by a keyword. Any patents you retrieve will break down into three parts. An introduction gives you a steer on why an invention or modification moves beyond the state of the art (which is essentially the level of development and knowledge achieved up to that point). A description then explains how the product or the process works, which is often accompanied by drawings. Finally, a series of claims are made which define the legal scope of what the patent protects. The initial claim is generally the broadest and most significant. Later ones will be more specific and conditional.

As you read the document, make sure you are aware of its status. If it is a published application, its claims will appear to be broad. If it is a granted patent, then the patent examiner is likely to have insisted on tighter and longer definitions. Remember, too, that not all patents are active – you are free to use these.

Under your own steam, you can go a long way towards mapping out your technological landscape. Before moving to the next stage, you may well want to ask the experts to check there are no patents hiding away in foreign databases and to advise on the extent of any claims that might be made against you.

Patents translate ideas into a legal property, so the language can become technical. It is always best to be sure that you are launching yourself into clear blue water.

To take your investigation to the next stage, try "patent mining". It is a technique that is gaining interest among venture capitalists and fund managers, who are waking up to the latent value in IP databases. First, you dig out the patents your competitors hold and then compare them to your own, spotting where any holes lie. You can then direct your research into exploring these holes and discovering gaps in existing technological practice.

Where next

www.ipo.gov.uk/types/patent/p-os/p-find.htm
www.carbonfirst.co.uk
www.umip.com
www.bl.uk/bipc/

Mark Thompson was formerly head of market development at the University of Manchester Intellectual Property Ltd, is now running his own consultancy focused on open innovation in the low carbon sector. Named by Intellectual Asset Management *magazine in 2009 as one of the world's top 250 IP Strategists. For further details email: mark.thompson@carbonfirst.co.uk.*

10

Academic to business networks

Simon Bond at Bath Ventures on how to make the right contacts

Networking is the lifeblood of business. Contacts are currency and connecting with like-minded people can yield information on new business opportunities, insight into what competitors are saying, or maybe a chance introduction to a potential new employee, employer or customer. Networking is not only a business phenomenon, universities thrive on it too. Peer-to-peer contact inside and outside universities provides information on new research contracts and trends, opportunities for researchers to find common interest and collaborate.

In an economy which needs business to become more competitive through innovation and which is asking universities to open up their research and natural creativity to make an economic impact, networking these two "worlds" together makes good sense.

The challenge is how we can increase their frequency and quality? How can we "engineer the serendipity" of the right people meeting each other at the right time and initiating a conversation on a topic that is most likely to lead to a positive commercial result?

In truth, engineering such a wide range of variables is maddeningly complex and couldn't be achieved by anything other than networks. In fact, to ensure that the many variable combinations of people and ideas are explored, an infrastructure or ecosystem of networks is a better solution – the cross-referencing, and inter-relationships between networks that are local, national, international, thematic, based on market sectors, and based on professional disciplines, is vital to yield the greatest likelihood of a valuable encounter.

It is possible to categorise networks, though often networks fall into more than one category – more useful is to look at the roles they serve.

Translation networks

There is clearly value in connecting entrepreneurially minded academics to business that values academic know-how and intellectual property. However, although there is mutual value and mutual respect, business and academia are wired differently. Business is driven by P&L (profit and loss) and ROI (return on investment), academics by FEC (full economic costing) and REF (Research Excellence Framework). So one role of networks is to translate, providing a platform for speakers to explain their interests and motivations and allow others to interpret how this can be used by them. This is particularly useful when considering really new science – it's easy to dismiss a new emerging technology as being "an invention looking for an application" and this may be the case, but it's only by networking with people who know how to commercially exploit ideas that you can find out if there really is a valuable application for it.

Common interest networks

Networks of common interest are like specialist magazines. Often grouped around vertical markets or a professional specialism, these networks provide a regular opportunity to "check in" with peers and like-minded people to find out what's going on, discuss trends and new opportunities. There's an often heard criticism of some networks that "it's filled with the same old faces". Sometimes this is no bad thing – the longevity and depth of relationships between like-minded people can produce extraordinary results.

Resource networks: "venture cannibalism"

Some people attend networking events with a shopping list – they're looking for an angel investor, a finance director or some programmers. A wonderful function of a free labour market is what I call "venture cannibalism" – creating a new business out of the bits, pieces and people that are locked up in a failing or stalled venture. Networking for resources means you can find the right resources that are in the wrong places and move them around. For example, a great CEO flogging a dead horse of a venture, could be more successful at raising seed funding if he or she were working on some university IP, perhaps technology which you have rights to in a hot new area? Networks provide the opportunity to "cannibalise" existing resources in the innovation sector and re-work them into something new and better. Such rapid re-engineering of people, resources and opportunities is key to increasing the clock-speed of innovation. Despite the cannibalism references, successful serial networkers will make sure that they give something back to the network that they go to for resources; after all they will get a bad reputation if they constantly leave nothing but bones.

Good networking

When networking works, it is wonderful – being "hooked up" with the right kind of people is empowering and makes you believe that anything is possible. Equally, there's nothing more soul destroying than being stuck in a room with a bunch of people you can find nothing in common with. Successful networks are those which are cognisant of how the participants can benefit each other and, like a good dinner party host, engineer the serendipity of valued and valuable connections. Here are some examples of useful, well managed networks.

Knowledge Transfer Networks

Created by the government's innovation agency, the Technology Strategy Board (TSB), the 15 or so Knowledge Transfer Networks each provide aspects of translation, like-minded connections and resources networks. Typically organised around market themes such as bioscience, materials or the creative industries, each KTN also provides information and access on the latest R&D grant funding opportunities available. Additionally, the KTNs are interlinked and the Technology Strategy Board has created a single over-arching national network which brings together people from businesses, universities, research, finance and technology organisations to stimulate innovation through knowledge transfer (https://ktn. innovateuk.org).

Start-up and innovation networks

To bring together the key players that help start-up ventures the Bath Ventures Innovation Centre has established a series of networks in high-growth areas. They're all free to join and shamelessly celebrate entrepreneurialism and the challenge of creating new businesses. For microelectronics entrepreneurs, the Silicon South West Network (www.siliconsouthwest.co.uk) publishes a regular newsletter reporting on new company developments in the sector and holds networking meetings where it invites entrepreneurs and investors to come and present. Similarly the Low Carbon South West Network (www.lowcarbonsouthwest.co.uk) focuses on cleantech and environmental technology; openMIC (http://open-mic.org.uk), the Mobile Innovation Camp brings together mobile apps developers with some of the major corporates in the mobile market to discuss mutual opportunities. Finally the Assisted Living Action Network (www.assistedlivingaction.net) provides a regular meeting spot for those interested in developing business opportunities in medtech and the massive global market for assisted living technology for the ageing population.

Regional networks

Of course no list of networks would be complete without reference to the Cambridge Network (www.cambridgenetwork.co.uk) which was one of the first and remains one of the most successful entrepreneurs' networks with close links to the university. Also, Cambridge Wireless (www.cambridgewireless.co.uk) has an unbeatable national and international reputation for its work in developing and promoting the region's highly successful wireless and mobile sector. In the South West, the Bath & Bristol Enterprise Network (www.bristolenterprise.com) similarly provides a regional focus for entrepreneurs and entrepreneurial academics to meet, mix and make the connections that will lead to the creation of new businesses.

Organisation profile

The SETsquared Partnership

The University of Bath is a member of another powerhouse of university company creation, the SETsquared Partnership. The group comprises the universities of Bath, Bristol, Exeter, Southampton and Surrey and it was formed to support high tech, high growth potential start-ups.

Between them, the universities boast 7,400 academics, 10% of the UK's higher education research budget and 90,000 students. Through its network of incubators, technology transfer offices and contacts, this group has produced 37 spin-outs, including six public market listings in the last five years valued at a combined £250m, and helped companies raise over £750m in funding.

SETsquared operates five Business Acceleration Centres on or near the universities' campuses and 90% of the ventures that have been incubated remain within its confines three years on. Start-ups that become involved with the partnership gain access to industry specialists, investors, business mentors and guidance, as well as physical office space.

The partnership also hosts an annual investment showcase in London, attended by more than 100 angel and venture capital investors. Companies pitching or exhibiting have access to an intensive investor readiness programme. In the last seven years companies that have attended the showcase have raised more than £100m in funding and in some cases have gained customer orders.

For businesses looking to grow internationally, the SETsquared Partnership has relationships with entrepreneur networks in San Diego and Boston in the US. To date, more than 200 technology companies have been supported in their global endeavours.

Simon Bond is head of Bath Ventures, the University of Bath's commercialisation group. He is Director of the University's Innovation Centre which, as part of the SETsquared Partnership, incubates technology start-ups. He leads the Bath Entrepreneurship Programme which provides personal development for entrepreneurs and founded the academic-to-business networks Silicon South West, for microelectronics start-ups; openMIC for mobile application developers; the Assisted Living Action Network for assisted living technology; and Low Carbon South West for new low carbon businesses. Contact 01225 388 682; s.a.bond@bath.ac.uk.

Looking for a patent attorney to add value to your university collaboration?

Company Statement by Dr Anton Hutter, Venner Shipley LLP

The value a patent attorney can add to your university collaborations

Whether you are a lone entrepreneur, or acting on behalf of an SME or a large multinational company, having the right patent attorney to help you navigate your way through the IP minefield is essential when embarking upon a knowledge transfer project.

This is particularly the case when it comes to university collaborations, due to the often sophisticated nature of the technologies concerned and the complexities of issues relating to ownership, licensing and portfolio management that can arise. Therefore, when choosing a patent attorney to assist you with such collaborations, it is important to check that they have experience of working with academics and university technology transfer executives. This helps to ensure you protect not only your IP rights, but also those of the university, thereby strengthening the collaboration, and making it a profitable business venture for all parties involved.

The patent attorney make-up

A patent attorney has a background comprising a mix of both scientific and legal training. Entrants into the patent profession must have, as a minimum, an undergraduate degree in a scientific or technical discipline, although many patent attorneys have postgraduate experience. This scientific background, which is a prerequisite for entry onto the register of both the European and UK patent institutes, ensures that your patent attorney is uniquely placed to appreciate the complex, technical aspects of your invention.

After entry into the profession, patent attorneys must then complete a minimum period of legal training (typically three to four years) before sitting rigorous professional examinations. Upon qualification, patent attorneys can therefore advise you in matters relating to all areas of IP, which includes patents, trademarks, design rights and copyright, as well as providing specific expertise on matters such as collaboration agreements, licensing and assignment of intellectual property rights, and patent portfolio management.

Establishing ownership

Even before a draft patent application defining your invention is prepared, it is important to ensure that the inventorship and ownership of the invention is clearly defined and, for this reason, it is often sensible to involve a patent attorney from the outset, to help protect your interests.

Ownership of IP rights can be a divisive issue, particularly where collaborative projects are concerned, since ownership may be rightfully shared across a number of different parties often having conflicting interests in the invention. Accurately designating the ownership of such inventions can be complicated, and it is therefore important to resolve these issues before filing a patent application order to avoid potentially significant and costly complications later on.

The patent application

Once these preliminary issues have been resolved, a patent attorney will usually begin by drafting a patent application describing your invention. A patent application is a complex legal document that must comply with a number of formal and substantive requirements, in order to produce a valid patent which will, when granted, protect your invention.

When carefully drafted, your patent application should cover both your current and any proposed commercial products, and be broad enough to cover minor or obvious modifications in order to act as a deterrent to potential competitors, while excluding things which have been done before.

Your attorney will liaise with you, the academics and the university technology transfer executives in order to ensure that the patent application is drafted in such a way so as to meet these goals and therefore be commercially relevant. Such a patent application should also prove attractive to a potential funding partner, thereby facilitating negotiations with third parties.

In order to obtain a valid patent in most countries of interest, the invention, as defined in your patent application, needs to meet three key requirements at its date of filing. First, it must be novel. This means that your invention must not have been made available to the public anywhere in the world, by any means, prior to the filing date of your patent application. An important aspect of novelty, therefore, is that your invention must remain strictly confidential until your patent application is safely on file.

Second, the invention must exhibit an inventive step, in the sense that it must not be merely an obvious development of what already exists in the public domain. If your invention exhibits any surprising advantages over known technology, then it is likely to involve an inventive step. Lastly, the invention must be susceptible of industrial application. This means that your invention must have utility in some kind of industry, or in agriculture. Your patent attorney will take these three criteria into consideration while preparing a draft patent application describing your invention.

These three requirements will ultimately be assessed by the relevant patent offices during examination of your patent application (also known as "prosecution"). In order to assess the patentability of your invention, therefore, each patent office will typically conduct a search of patent and scientific literature in the field of your invention, in order to determine what was known at the time of filing your patent application.

This so-called "prior art" will then form the basis of the patent examination. In order to better understand how your patent application is likely to be viewed, therefore, your patent attorney might suggest conducting a novelty search prior to filing your patent application to look for any such information which could negatively impact on the patentability of your invention, and advise you on the potential implications for the scope of protection that you can expect to achieve.

Formal requirements

In addition to these substantive requirements, a patent application must also meet several formal requirements, which, again, your patent attorney will bear in mind when preparing your draft patent application. For example, the patent application must contain enough information to describe the invention in sufficient detail so that it can be repeated by a third party without them having to exercise their own inventive endeavour.

Furthermore, it must be plausible that the technical advantages ascribed to your invention can be achieved on the basis of the information included in the patent application on the date it is filed. Your patent attorney will therefore carefully consider whether you have generated enough data to support the claimed invention as formally required.

Sometimes, it may be prudent for you to wait for a period of time before filing your patent application, if your attorney believes that more data should be obtained first. Timing is critical, because filing either too soon or too late can, under certain circumstances, put the validity of your patent application at risk, thereby compromising its value.

Filing the patent

Once the wording of your draft patent application has been agreed, your patent attorney will then file it at the patent office. Depending on your commercial interests, this may be the UK Intellectual Property Office or the European Patent Office (or even, in certain cases, a patent office in another jurisdiction, such as the US).

The filing date of your patent application is all important, as this is the date at which the relevant patent offices will determine whether your application meets the substantive requirements for grant. This essentially means that any prior art which was filed after your filing date, will not be relevant for determining the patentability of your invention. Therefore, once your patent application is safely on file you can disclose your invention to third parties, in an attempt to gain interest in, and generate revenue via, the technology.

Securing additional territories

Patents are territorial in nature, and so, in order to protect your invention in other jurisdictions, it is necessary to file a patent application in each country of interest. In order to allow patentees sufficient time in which to do so, any qualifying patent application for the same invention which is filed within 12 months of your initial UK or European patent application can claim "priority".

This means that, subject to compliance with the priority provisions, the later foreign applications will benefit from the filing date of the initial application and, as for the initial application, any prior art published in the intervening 12 months, will not be relevant to the patentability of your invention.

Extending an initial application to other territories is generally done in one of two ways: either by filing national patent applications directly in the other countries of interest, or by filing an international patent application under the Patent Co-operation Treaty (PCT). There are a large number of factors to be taken into account when deciding which of these routes to follow, and therefore this decision should always be made in conjunction with strategic advice from your patent attorney.

Negotiating amendments

Once your patent application has been filed, the various national patent offices will search and examine it in order to assess whether or not your invention is indeed novel, inventive and industrially applicable, and many patent offices will also judge your patent application for the sufficiency and supporting data requirements.

At this stage, your patent attorney will report the official search and examination reports to you, and advise you on the impact that any cited documents may have against your patent application. Using a clear understanding of your commercial drivers, your attorney can then suggest amendments that may need to be made to the wording of your patent application in order to distinguish your invention over the cited prior art, with the aim of achieving the broadest possible scope of protection, while ensuring that this still covers your commercial products.

This "negotiation" with the patent offices usually involves only written communication, but for more complex cases, it can require an interview or formal hearing with the patent office examiner or an examination board, at which arguments in support of the invention's patentability can be orally submitted.

Granting of a patent and beyond

Finally, once a consensus on the scope of protection afforded by your patent application is reached with the patent office, your patent will then be ready for grant. By this time, it is hoped that either you and/or the university will have found a way of making money out of the invention. For example, revenue could be generated by selling the patent outright to a third party, or, alternatively, the technology could be licensed under the patent, to one or more competitors in exchange for licensing fees. At Venner Shipley, we can draw up detailed IP reports, which describe your IP portfolio, and can be used to attract potential investors and/or business partners.

The role of a patent attorney does not end when your patent is granted, however. For example, as time goes by, you may further develop your invention, and it can often be advantageous to your business to also protect these refinements. Your attorney will advise you on the patentability of the developments, and ensure that they are adequately protected by filing one or more subsequent patent applications, which more specifically define your commercial products. Additionally, filing so-called "improvement" patents can extend the length of patent protection and avoid a dramatic slump in revenue at the end of patent life.

When a commercial product is particularly successful, third parties may try to take advantage of the underlying concept on which your invention is based by selling a competing product. In such situations, you will need your patent attorney to advise whether or not that competing product falls within the scope of your patent, ie "infringes" your patent in a certain jurisdiction.

In the event that your patent is being infringed, your attorney can take steps to restrict the actions of the infringer, for example by taking action before the Patents County Court (PCC) in the UK to obtain an injunction and/or damages from the infringing party. For more complex cases, patent attorneys often work in conjunction with IP solicitors and barristers to take action in the High Court, and your attorney can instruct and liaise with these specialists on your behalf. If legal action is to be taken in another jurisdiction, your foreign patents can be litigated by local IP professionals, again under instructions from your patent attorney.

Alternatively, you may wish to determine whether your own product risks infringing any third party patents (whether or not your product is protected by a patent) before bringing it to market. In such a scenario, your patent attorney can search for competing patents, and advise you whether or not your activities would be likely to constitute an infringement, if litigated.

If it is likely that it would infringe a competitor's patent, your patent attorney can assist you in taking pre-emptive action, for example by carrying out due diligence on that patent in order to determine whether or not it is valid. Your attorney can also propose tactics for having the earlier patent invalidated or restricted, or, if necessary, help you to negotiate a deal with the patentee in order to enable you to legally bring your product to market.

In summary, it is vital that you choose the correct patent attorney to join you on your voyage of collaboration with a university. They need to have the relevant scientific background so that they can understand your invention, be experienced in dealing with academics and university technology transfer departments, and have the ability to give complex legal advice using jargon-free language.

Dr Anton Hutter is a UK and European patent attorney, and is a partner in the Chemical & Life Sciences team of Venner Shipley LLP, a firm of patent and trade mark attorneys with offices in London and Cambridge; www.vennershipley.co.uk.

PART 3
Access to talent

Tom Greveson of Revolution Viewing, a Goldman Sachs *10,000 Small Businesses* programme graduate, with Rob Whieldon, of Leeds University Business School

GENERATING
BUSINESS LEEDS

To find out more about working with the University of Leeds contact:

business@leeds.ac.uk
0113 3430900
www.leeds.ac.uk/business

UNIVERSITY OF LEEDS

11

How to find an expert

How to solve real-world challenges by asking an academic

You can easily find yourself asking the right question without knowing where to start finding an answer. At this point, it often pays to draw on the advice of someone who spends their working life reviewing the state of the art in your field and studying the directions in which it might move next.

Rob Blackwell had reached this point, and like many of us had never thought about turning to the university up the road. He assumed it was an ivory tower closed to the outside world and just concerned with teaching.

As head of research and development at Advanced Web Solutions (AWS) in Ipswich, Blackwell spends his time resolving knotty problems in how to share information for major players such as Microsoft. On this occasion, he found himself struggling with a particularly awkward question from the construction industry.

On projects, contractors are being held more and more tightly to account. It is an expectation that can last for years. Put up a building, for instance. If the sprinkler system then fails after five years, you still have to explain why.

Normally, it means digging deep back into records, which can take time in an industry where numerous suppliers are involved. If an easier way of retrieving this mass of correspondence could be found it would be highly attractive, particularly when the regulator is waiting for an answer.

How about if you could create an intelligent filter, which automatically intercepts emails, making a judgment on their relevance on the first pass and creating an intelligent database? It was no more than a good thought, when a colleague suggested that Blackwell have a chat with the university where she had been working.

Blackwell had no expectations, so his initial meeting with Udo Kruschwitz and Simon Lucas at the School of Computer Science and Engineering at the University of Essex caught him by surprise. First, he was impressed by how ready they were to tackle challenges in the real world as the basis for their teaching and research. Second, he found that Kruschwitz was working on two areas that related directly to his search for an intelligent database: natural language engineering for automatically reading correspondence such as emails and enterprise search as a method for categorising information.

How, he was asking, do you keep track of a complex project such as the Olympics where you have numerous contractors working over a number of years? As we know, it can all go expensively wrong. If you could automatically track the links between them, you could query the database and quickly see the state of play at any point in time. At least, that was Kruschwitz's theory.

"I had no idea that we had such an intellectual powerhouse on the doorstep," says Blackwell. Almost immediately, he found himself discussing the scope for an assignment to apply this expertise in extracting knowledge from documents.

The mechanism that they chose was a Knowledge Transfer Partnership (KTP) which is a programme designed to apply a university's expertise to the challenges that a business is facing in developing innovative solutions. A new product, a new service or a new process might be the result.

Typically, each assignment lasts for one to three years. A graduate is recruited and employed by the university, but will then work full time in your business under the supervision of a senior academic such as Kruschwitz or Lucas. As an enterprise, you meet a third of the cost. The rest is covered by a fund organised centrally through the Technology Strategy Board.

For SMEs, there is an option to run shorter programmes of 10 to 40 weeks, although you can review your involvement after three months on longer programmes. After a recent confirmation that the scheme will continue as an integral part of the government's commitment to accelerating innovation, you can also qualify to pay 25% instead of 33% of the cost.

The scheme has been running for over 30 years and typically funds well over a thousand projects each year. All forms of commercial activity are included. As well as computer science, Essex has run projects in areas as diverse as biology, psychology, law and theatre studies.

The calculation is that the cost for an SME is significantly lower than recruiting a new member of staff directly. As well as bringing a researcher into the business to work on a problem for you, you gain access to the university's knowledge of your field as a whole.

Even though it appeared to be a no-brainer for AWS, it still represented a serious investment and Blackwell had to satisfy his board that any risks were limited. It was a piece of research AWS would have undertaken anyway, he argued, so why not work with the credibility of an organisation such as Essex? The other consideration was all the potential spin-offs in building a strong relationship with the School of Computer Science and Engineering as a source of expertise, as well as a source of new talent.

Kruschwitz then submitted a proposal for a two-year assignment to run from May 2008 to May 2010. Once the funds were approved, Dyaa Albakour was taken on as the KTP research associate.

Looking back, the benefits have been huge, says Blackwell. A prototype has been developed, but, following the downturn, it is still waiting to be commercialised. All AWS's customers are aware of these new features, which are being built into its future strategy. One unexpected side effect is that the relationship with Essex has led to a change in how AWS is perceived and more value is given to their commitment to R&D.

On the back of the KTP, AWS is now running placements for students from Essex each year and gets first pick when they graduate. During the year, Blackwell appears as a guest lecturer and continues to drop into the department when he has another problem to crack.

For the university, the relationship has proved equally beneficial, although in a different way. Says Blackwell: "We can now tell students that we are working in the real world and that they have the chance to gain direct commercial experience."

On the basis of the KTP research, the school has appeared in several academic publications: "It is essential to show that we are active at the cutting edge."

The KTP associate, Dyaa Albakour, has since enrolled on a PhD at the school and is now working with Kruschwitz on another research project.

Would AWS consider repeating the experience? Absolutely, says Blackwell.

> *"You have to find the right people with the right expertise. You have to align the KTP to your business, so it is well planned and targeted.*
>
> *For us, it turned into a really positive experience. KTPs are exactly what the business should be doing to get out of recession and put UK plc back on its feet."*

Creative design

At festivals and among students, word was spreading about the clothes designed and made by Funzee. The worry for the label's owner, Mark Heselgrave, was to get the sizes right to cut down on the number of returns being made.

So he called in Denise Ward, a tutor in fashion production at the University for the Creative Arts, which specialises as a leader in art, design, architecture, media and communication. She had spent 13 years as production manager at Karen Millen, the fashion designer, so knew all about the problems Mark was experiencing and created a more scientific method of dealing with sizing.

"I introduced a height-based policy, which standardised Funzee's offer," she says, "and created a user-friendly information table for the website."

"Because of Denise's advice," says Heselgrave, "our return rate has been much reduced, as people are now buying the size that is correct for them."

With a proper foundation in sizing, Heselgrave is gaining the confidence to research other ranges of clothing and launch new products, although he continues to draw on Ward's expertise on a variety of issues, including fabrics, production specifications and processes.

12

Recruiting students and graduates

How to make use of placements, internships and competitions

Looking for flexible, intelligent individuals to crack a technical challenge, create a new marketing channel or improve your operational performance? Then consider talking to the careers centre at a university.

You might think it only runs a service for corporates and the professions. You might expect to have to fit into the academic calendar. In fact, as a smaller company, it is possible for you to ring up a university at any time of the year and ask about bringing in someone on the shorter schedules to which you are used to working.

All told, there are 2.5 million students and graduates within higher education in the UK, so you have a vast pool of talent on which to draw. You can look at several different ways to bring the right person on board and the university will help you run the recruitment process for free.

Full-time posts are the conventional route, of course. But most enterprises will prefer to try someone out first. The risk of taking on an IT graduate at £25,000 a year or a marketing assistant at £15,000 might be too much of a risk.

Depending on the scope of your project, you could think about a part-time contract. At universities such as Manchester, students are free to work up to 20 hours a week and many will be looking to work during their three months of summer holiday.

Anne Milligan in the careers and employability division at Manchester University says:

> "Students are flexible in the role they can perform and the hours they can work. They can think tasks through, will communicate well and are used to working in teams. Some will want to work with large employers, of course. Others who want to stay in the region or set up their own business will be attracted to smaller companies."

To maximise the potential of shorter term assignments, you might look at three schemes that universities run: placements, internships and competitions.

Placements

Originally, placements were when students spent one year of their degree working directly for a company outside the university. Today, the principle is being expanded into shorter projects of four to 12 weeks in which students can apply their specialist knowledge within a commercial setting.

One enterprise that is adopting this model is Save Me A Ticket. Founded and run by Qumar Haq as a way of exchanging tickets, it lets you buy and sell them securely. To improve his marketing, he set up two placements through the University of East London.

One was to bring the company's presence on social media up to speed. The other was to improve its online marketing through blogs, press releases, articles and video clips. Both roles had an offline element in attending events to promote the company.

Haq says:

> "I wanted candidates who had a good knowledge of the internet as well as having good written skills, an interest in music and with a good personality.
>
> It is a really good scheme. It gives students a stepping stone into work. We can see what students without previous experience but with a lot of passion can deliver. So far the projects have met all my needs and exceeded my expectations."

Internships

Internships can be another cost-effective vehicle for SMEs to gain a highly qualified resource in the short term. To gain commercial experience and apply their specialist knowledge, more and more graduates are working on short-term contracts. These internships generally last four to 12 months.

At Manchester, Anne Milligan and her colleagues at the careers centre work closely with companies to match a task to the right candidate. Of the 70 interns she places a year, most are with SMEs.

The programme is in its fourth year and is going from strength to strength. "We have a pool of graduates waiting," says Milligan. "Many will be coming off short-term contracts and are looking for their next challenge, so you can run ideas past us all year round."

As well as working directly with universities, SMEs can work through private intermediaries, such as www.enternships.com and www.inspiringinterns.com, as a way of bringing interns into the company.

Competitions

Pashley Cycles has found another way of drawing on the ingenuity of students. In business since 1926, it produces hand-built bikes and trikes.

One of its classic designs, The Guv'nor, is a retro 1930s racer, which many cycling enthusiasts use at vintage rallies. In looking to develop new accessories for this model, Pashley turned to Birmingham City University.

Within their course, students at the Institute for Art and Design were asked to adapt the aesthetics and technology for parts such as water bottles, repair kits, mudguards, bells and pumps. The best 22 concepts appeared in an exhibition.

Adrian William, managing director at Pashley, was so "blown away" by the calibre and authenticity of what he saw that he offered a design contract to one of the graduates from the school.

Process

To secure such outcomes, the careers centres at universities such as Manchester and East London are happy to work with SMEs for free.

Once a request is made, they will assess the skills that are actually required, deciding whether it translates into a full-time, part-time or short-term role. They then write the job description and circulate it to students and graduates. Often, they find themselves processing the applications and drawing up a shortlist.

At Manchester, Milligan likes to visit potential employers if possible, but generally only goes to those considering internships. But in putting forward an opening at an SME, she will always highlight why it might be attractive to students. Is it producing innovative products? Has it won any awards? What is the profile of the managing director? For her, no post is one size fits all. It is in the university's interests for it to be right for both the student and the employer.

Internships: potential into reality

Ellie Taplin is an architecture graduate from the University of Brighton. She was unemployed and looking for real graduate work experience in her home town of Norwich. She had engaged with local company Artarchitecture but it was unable to offer her paid work as it is a small business and unable to afford to bring graduate level skills into the organisation.

Artarchitecture heard about the HEFCE funded programme for graduate internships through its membership of the Federation of Small Businesses. The company contacted the University of Brighton, which was able to support both its graduate and the business as part of the programme.

Annabel Lockhart of Artarchitecture found that the initial engagement with the University and general recruitment process went smoothly and that the support from the internships officer was invaluable: "She made sure we had all the information and ensured we were able to contact her if we had any queries etc. She made sure everything was going well." She also found Ellie "very, very good quality, very knowledgeable and willing to work hard".

In feedback to the University, the business said that the involvement with the programme "certainly met our expectations and [...] opened up opportunities for both us and the intern. Yes, we would consider being part of another internship programme. The interns are willing to learn and work hard which is great. The staff were very helpful and friendly."

13

Sponsoring a PhD

How to use doctorates to accelerate growth

As head of forensics at West Midlands Police, Richard Leary squeezed in a doctorate around his life at work and at home. His four years of research into how to optimise systems for investigations proved a cathartic experience for him.

First, it showed how much you could achieve when you put your mind to it. Second, it propelled him into setting up his own business, Forensic Pathways.

Since 2003, it has been growing at a steady 20%–30% a year. From its base in Tamworth, Staffordshire, it now employs 17 people who work on assignments for those looking for new patterns in large quantities of data in the police, the law and telecoms.

Drawing on his experience at University College London, Leary decided to fund a series of PhDs as part of his growth plan:

> "It is a great way of developing intellectual property and finding the best people. You immediately find yourself at the edge of innovation. Instead of trying to catch up, it is you that is taking the lead. Yes, it means working with disruptive technologies and you have to carve out new markets where none existed before, but you put yourself in a position to accelerate your growth."

The next PhD for completion is on forensic ballistics which has been run with the University of Huddersfield. Although it is being launched in three months, it is already making a commercial impact and the student is managing a major contract for Forensic Pathways, as well as putting the finishing touches to her thesis.

Set-up

So far, Leary has sponsored seven PhDs, each costing him around £100,000 for a three-year programme. Only one has been supported by a grant.

In finding projects to pursue, he regularly visits universities and gives talks on entrepreneurship. He then either raises an idea or the university asks him about sponsoring a programme. So far, he has worked with Warwick, Birmingham City, Keele, Staffordshire and Birmingham, as well as Huddersfield.

Be careful in your selection process, he says.

> *"Don't just go to the first one. In particular, look at the track record for whoever is going to supervise the research. See whether they have any experience of industry. If they just operate in the lecture theatre, forget it. They will have no idea about commercial exploitation."*

The relationship

When you find the right academic to work on a project, collaborations can be highly rewarding, but you still need to watch your relationship with the university, says Leary. He has had some disappointing experiences.

First, universities tend to move at their own pace. Second, you can find a disconnect between your objectives. "If it is just a question of raising money to fund research activities, then run away. Your partners have to be interested in the project if you are going to collaborate."

Even then, make sure you read any contracts carefully. "Some assume, you will stump up the money and they will see you in three years' time. Watch out as well for any clause that says the university can pull out at any point it wants."

In all the discussions he has had, Leary has found that the newer universities are often hungrier for growth and more willing to collaborate.

On-site

The main point of contention is usually Leary's insistence that the research students come and work on-site at Forensic Pathways. He believes that these are applied PhDs, which should be pursued like any other job.

"We develop a new area. The student gets a doctorate and a guaranteed job. We don't want anyone just sitting around on campus."

His other reason is that three years can be too long to spend on research, before then considering how to exploit the results. "Your window will disappear. You have to get the commercial wheels turning."

Intellectual property

The assumption is often made that the university is creating the IP. In fact, in Leary's experience, the IP is developed within the company with the student. He says:

> "We ask a stretching question, then conduct the research to find the answer.
>
> What the university brings is the discipline of rigorous academic study, not the idea itself. So we protect the IP as we go along and pay the university a royalty on any exploitation.
>
> If they do want to retain the IP, my response is to ask them to pay the costs of patenting, then assume the responsibility for managing and enforcing it, exercising a duty of care towards us. At that point, they generally back off."

The ideas pipeline

As a route to growth, Leary definitely recommends sponsoring PhDs. As well as the programme on forensic ballistics, he has three other projects that are close to market: a digital signature to track photos taken on mobile phones; an index to identify links between the millions of images held on a database; and a system for the intelligent processing of large quantities of telecoms data.

Underpinned by these innovations, Leary is confident that his company can continue its steady growth of 20%–30% a year. His strategy is to act as if Forensic Pathways is already a big company in terms of its operations, branding and recruitments. "Our PhDs are part of that. They help us to stand out from the crowd."

Leary's rules for PhD collaborations

- Universities excel in bringing rigour and discipline to your research.

- PhDs accelerate your innovation and help you find top talent.

- Collaborations can work brilliantly, but be careful which university you select – don't just go to the first one.

- Find an academic to supervise a project who knows how the commercial world works.

- For applied PhDs, insist on the student coming to work for you.

- Set the commercial wheels in motion early, don't wait on the results.

- Companies know best how to manage and exploit the commercial rights.

- Pay the university a royalty on the IP you take to market.

14

Workforce development

How to work with universities to translate learning at work into skills for growth

As a student, the highly structured qualification you gain is the gold standard for entering the workforce. Paradoxically, once you become an employee, you often leave behind this model of learning. The training you then undertake is usually geared towards integrating you into a company's culture and building a team. Later, it will help you take on more responsibility and develop you as a leader.

As Professor Simon Roodhouse at Middlesex University argues in a new book, *Understanding Work Based Learning* (Gower, 2010), graduates tend to lose track of their learning progression and academics find it hard to relate to the style of in-house training.

Traditionally, he says, academics have believed that: "Legitimate and verifiable learning can only take place within the confines of the campus. By the same token, those in full-time employment ... begin to see the academic alternative as out of touch, esoteric and lacking relevance."

The trouble is that such attitudes can lead to a failure to capture the value that lies in the knowledge that is being created within a commercial setting, as well as all the on-the-job learning that takes place. For smaller companies, however, it is becoming possible to combine the best of both worlds at relatively low cost. In the process of developing solutions and improving performance, employees now have the chance to gain a qualification recognised and validated by a university at the same time. For a business that is looking to prosper and grow, there are some distinct advantages.

- You combine the pragmatism of work with academic rigour.
- You work on real projects that correspond to your commercial objectives.
- You set the direction that the learning will take.
- You bring theory and operational practice together.
- Your workplace learners start to behave like graduates.
- You can include those with a wealth of practical knowledge, but few formal qualifications.
- You can set up a learning escalator from an introductory qualification up to a master's degree.

The challenge still lies in overcoming old prejudices and making such work-based learning happen. Many universities are already designing courses that reflect what employers require. Others are spearheading more innovative learning solutions.

These changes are being supported by £150m from the HEFCE in a programme that is running from 2008–12. The goal is to encourage growth by building relationships between universities and businesses to develop skills.

Many universities now have someone who specialises in finding out what businesses need and who then reaches back into the university to tailor modules and programmes. By 2010, 7,000 employees from SMEs were participating in such courses and numbers are continuing to grow.

The convention that a university must exercise full control over the content of any learning is being moderated. As an employer, your priorities can be reflected in a number of ways. Examples include the following.

- **The co-funded model** supported by HEFCE to create flexible courses based on what employers have requested. Under the current programme, HEFCE will help subsidise each learner, although you will be expected to make a contribution towards costs either in cash or in kind, such as the use of your premises or letting your staff teach.
- **Foundation degrees**, which have been running since 2000 to cut the shortage of intermediate skills and prepare students for work. More recently, some larger companies, such as Tesco, have put recruits through their own version of these degrees in partnership with a university.

- **University validation**, in other cases, such as the degree run by McDonalds, a university validates a course and checks it for quality, but does not design its content.

When it comes to SMEs in particular, universities such as Huddersfield are adopting frameworks for continuing professional development, which allow participants to choose relevant modules from across the university and to combine these to create their own programme of study.

Kevin Orr at Huddersfield University's School for Education and Professional Development says:

"Whether an SME needs training on the impact of new legislation, on innovative technologies or on cutting-edge research, universities can provide it. Through highly focused provision or through other broader courses, universities help people to develop themselves and their companies by combining academic rigour with professional experience."

The old patterns of full time, part time or distance learning on a set schedule are also breaking down. At the University of Derby, a more flexible approach is being adopted, says Charles Hancock, a workforce development fellow at the university:

"We recognise that our delegates are very busy individuals. SMEs have many pressures which are not only financial but generally time-based. To ensure that delegates get the best value from their learning experience, we offer various opportunities to enable the delegate to achieve their required learning outcomes. One particular way of engaging with learners is by using bite-sized sessions that build up a portfolio over time. As learner, you can manage your own time in a way that fits into the busy schedule of operating a new or growing enterprise.

Bite-sized modules can be supplemented with additional online learning modules that are specific to your own learning needs. In each case, a partnership develops that corresponds to each learner's own personal development plan."

Further details: HEFCE provides funding to universities and HE colleges to undertake knowledge exchange and workforce development activity, working with businesses. Companies interested in finding out more about what universities are able to offer should contact their local university or college directly.

On its page for employers (www.hefce.ac.uk/econsoc/employer/), links and information are given for those wishing to find out which university or college can help support development of their staff. Employer engagement funded projects focused on the development and delivery of HE programmes co-funded by employers are also listed alphabetically by lead organisation.

Live learning

Cameron Measurements, an engineering SME based in West Sussex, identified the need to raise the skills levels of managers in the company. The company approached the University of Chichester which proposed the existing Foundation Degree in Business and Management as a vehicle for this training.

Cameron Measurements identified four members of its staff who would be appropriate to undertake training at this level. The employer did not want to commit staff to a full Foundation Degree and felt that it had some clear areas of focus for the training. The university worked with the employer to develop the content and delivery methods to create a bespoke, sector specific programme that met the learning needs of the individual learners and their employer.

The result was a series of five modules leading to the achievement of 75 credits, which can be carried forward into the Foundation Degree at a later date if either the learners or the business decide to take this further. A key element of this programme is the work-based learning activity where learners work on live projects within the workplace enabling the organisation to benefit from the learning as it takes place.

Value of work-based learning for the employer

According to Professor Simon Roodhouse at Middlesex University, the value of work-based learning and accreditation to the employer can be summarised in the following ways.

- Employees undertake real work in company projects which are of direct benefit to the organisation.
- It realises the intellectual capital of the company.
- It encourages self-confidence by recognising individual experience and accrediting it.
- It provides a means of measuring the performance of externally purchased training programmes through assessment.
- Minimum loss of work time, it is not campus-based.

- Increased loyalty results from the visible investment in the development of the workforce.

- Staff retention rates are improved and enhanced capabilities of existing workforce can help with recruitment, both as a means of attracting new employees, but also as a means of promoting from within the organisation.

- Organisations can work with a university to develop a tailor-made award which supports the individual professional development of employees but also reflects organisational priorities.

- Organisational and cultural change can be supported through work-based learning projects.

- Work-based learning is a means of addressing strategic business objectives and meeting an organisation's business plans.

- Employers and employees are in the driving seat taking control of their learning.

Further details: Professor Simon Roodhouse, Institute for Work Based Learning, Middlesex University, tel: 07810 200 202.

Local growth skills

In July 2011, the University of Bedfordshire's Knowledge Hub was awarded funding, to deliver a Higher Level Skills for Growth programme. The free programme of personal development and business training is for employees in key sectors of the Bedfordshire economy and will provide a series of short, bite-sized, training workshops coupled with masterclasses to develop the necessary skills to support innovation in business.

The programme will focus on innovation, business growth, business change and improvement. Funding for the programme has come from Central Bedfordshire and Bedford Borough Councils and the European Social Fund.

Employees must live in Bedfordshire and be engaged in employment by SMEs or be working in public, not-for profit or voluntary sector organisations. The course will take place in the evenings and last 12 weeks starting in January 2012. The key academic partner in this new Knowledge Hub project is the University's Business School "Centre for Leadership Innovation" which will provide the academic input and delivery in collaboration with its other partners.

Rita Mascia, business development manager in the Knowledge Hub, said: "Skills development has long been recognised as one of the five drivers of productivity alongside and linked with competition, entrepreneurship, innovation and investment. This project will provide higher level skills to managers in Bedfordshire whose companies are ready to grow and innovate."

Newcastle University
Business School

EFMD
EQUIS
ACCREDITED

Accredited by
Association
of MBAs

A world-class home
for business education

**Work with
our people
to unlock new
perspectives
on your
business**

**Dr Joanna Berry
Director of Engagement**

joanna.berry@ncl.ac.uk

**Boost your
career with
an
internationally
accredited
executive MBA**

**Juli Campey
Director, Executive
MBA Programme**

juli.campey@ncl.ac.uk

A
New
Perspective

www.ncl.ac.uk/nubs   You can find us on:

15

Business advice

Universities can help take an enterprise through the growth cycle

You might realistically expect to talk to a university about making an innovation, solving a technical issue or bringing a specialist on board. It is less likely that you will ask them how to tackle any of the practical challenges that you face in building and growing your business.

Yet universities are starting to move in this direction. In the case of the University of Hertfordshire, which has taken over the local Business Link, there is an explicit commitment to giving business advice to local SMEs. Other universities are developing schemes and programmes to help you move forward through each stage of growth from start-up to becoming a competitive force in your market.

At the start, you can get yourself up to speed by taking a part-time course in business and management in the evenings or at weekends. For improvements which you might otherwise find economically unviable or for expertise which you would normally be unable to obtain, universities are now actively engaged in looking at how they can set up projects for you which are funded wholly or in part by schemes such as a short-term Knowledge Transfer Partnership or an innovation voucher.

When you start

One start-up that got itself up to speed through a course is Bea's of Bloomsbury, an independent café and pastry shop, which has now become one of the worst-kept secrets in foodie London. Owner-manager Bea Vo trained as a pastry chef in acclaimed restaurants such as Nobu and Asia de Cuba before setting up her business in 2008 with just two full-time employees, including herself.

Since completing the Starting Up in Business course at City University, Bea has expanded her business to employ some 22 staff and has recently opened a second outlet within the prestigious One New Change shopping centre opposite St Paul's Cathedral in London.

When you improve

To improve its chance of winning contracts for its green educational products, Ecostyle in Luton wanted to adopt international standards as a set of robust procedures to prove itself when it came in front of potential buyers.

For help, it turned to the Knowledge Hub, the gateway to business at the University of Bedfordshire, which was running a scheme last year designed to result in greater efficiency, higher profits, better decisions or more jobs within local SMEs. Funded through the regional development agency, these innovation vouchers made up to £3,000 available for one-to-one consultancy assignments.

So far, the university has worked on 22 of these assignments. According to the consultancy manager at the Knowledge Hub, Veronica Rigby, the scheme is creating "an excellent platform for businesses in the region to access the university's expertise in addressing real business issues".

When you grow

On a larger scale, you can recruit a university to take your business to a new dimension. In 1998, for instance, Addison Lee was a medium-sized car service with 800 vehicles within the M25. Its operations were manual, using radio systems to speak to drivers. If it was going to keep growing, it accepted that it would need a total makeover.

Help and inspiration came from the University of Westminster which proposed a complete IT infrastructure rebuilt from scratch within a Knowledge Transfer

Partnership. For Addison Lee, the financial risks were relatively low. In today's terms, such a two-year programme costs £120,000, two-thirds of which is covered by a grant to the university.

The design that Westminster's School of Computer Science proposed was to be an enabler, giving Addison Lee the building blocks to take itself forward in quantum leaps, as and when it was ready. By acquiring this expertise in data storage and complex engineering techniques, the telephonists at Addison Lee could start to communicate more easily and accurately with their fleet. As well as leaving their competitors far behind, the system has been able to keep pace with the company's growth.

Addison Lee now has 2,600 cars and it can track all of them. That means it can reach the driver most suitable for any journey, while letting the passenger know exactly how long it will take for the car to arrive, accounting for weather and traffic conditions.

Addison Lee's new communication infrastructure.

Depending on your inclination and your age, you can order a car however you like. A friendly voice is there for those who prefer personal contact, but 40% of bookings are made through Facebook, iPhone and other apps – without needing to speak to a call centre.

The result? Average pick-up times have halved from 20 minutes to 10 minutes, and the company is 10 times more profitable than it was before it re-designed the platform on which it ran its operations.

16

Executive education for SMEs

Hina Wadhwa-Gonfreville and Dawn Bournand at QS discuss the programmes that can take managers to the next level

Entrepreneurs often create a company around what they love and do best, but running a successful business requires more than just passion. Small and medium-sized business owners must understand the range of competencies that is required of them: from IT to marketing, human resources to finance. An Executive MBA degree or Executive Education programme allows an entrepreneur/owner to get this much needed broader perspective.

It is also beneficial for SME owners and managers to understand where their strengths and weaknesses lie. This will enable them to fill in the gaps. Strategy, marketing and accounting are some of the most common areas where those in the SME driving seat can use a bit of help – unless, of course, this is the company's own area of expertise!

Executive MBA degrees (EMBA) and certain executive education classes include coursework specifically on these and other segments of a modern day business. In addition, executive education classes will also cover what are commonly known as soft skills; topics such as leadership, personality traits, social graces, communication and optimism that characterise relationships with other people. These skills have proven to be vital in keeping employees satisfied while building up a loyal client base – the key to any successful business.

In the past, business schools have traditionally catered to the needs of large corporations. In recent years, however, small companies have also resorted to executive education and work-related training as a retention tool for key employees. In the UK, for example, salary sacrifice schemes which benefit both the employer and employee, have contributed to the increase of SME managers in business school classrooms. Business schools and universities have also updated their curricula and offer courses specifically addressing SME and family business management. Managers learn how to rethink and benchmark their strategy, as well as create innovation and idea management pipelines – vital for retaining competitive advantage in the marketplace.

Local universities and business schools offer a variety of services to SMEs, including helping business owners and managers define the training programme best suited to the needs of the company. SMEs can also get acquainted with business school offerings by proposing a consultancy project to MBA and EMBA participants (a compulsory part of the curriculum) or by attending conferences organised by local education providers.

Taking management to the next level: understanding and working with strengths and weaknesses

The time for continuing education will vary for each person, but it is wise for small business owners to analyse their business and ask themselves if they or their key managers are knowledgeable enough to take it to the next level.

If there is any doubt whatsoever, it is time to consider some form of executive education.

Executive education can play a key role in the development and growth of an enterprise, yet many small business owners and SME managers are unaware of the potential such an education can bring.

The market offerings are vast, not only in terms of the number of business schools delivering such programmes, but also the types of courses offered and their format.

From local business schools to the big brands of the management education industry, it's a daunting task for any entrepreneur to decide which programme best suits his or her needs. Moreover, there is a general misconception that business schools mainly accommodate the needs of large corporations to train and retain top management.

The landscape of management education is in transformation, as we see a growing number of participants with non-business backgrounds appearing in Executive MBA classrooms. NGO executives, doctors, lawyers, architects as well as entrepreneurs or SME managers are all seeing the value of going back to school, but why?

Whether it's a two-year Executive MBA programme or a two-day executive education workshop, owners and managers can acquire the skills necessary to move their business forward, such as the following.

- Viewing the company as an interdependent whole and not as separate, dislocated units that function independently.

- Assessing the impact of one's managerial style and how to get employees/colleagues/teams to work as one towards a goal.

- Learning how to make decisions based not just on instinct or intuition, but also backing them up with figures and facts.

Designed around your business commitments

Unlike the required schedule for pursuing a full-time MBA degree, weekend and modular programmes are very typical for the Executive MBA. Executive education workshops, licences and degrees can be even more flexible as they are often shorter and specifically worked around attendees' schedules.

The learning period is not only stimulating for the participant but it can also be very beneficial for their employees or colleagues, as they too benefit indirectly from the new ideas and knowledge. It is during this time that owners and managers, who are busy studying, can begin to implement their succession planning. Top employees can be recognised and given new responsibilities and projects while the boss is spending extra time on studies.

Executive education programmes can also work well for female candidates who may be juggling family commitments alongside a mix of work, study and social activities. Executive programmes take this into account and work to create study programmes that are complementary to professional and personal lives. As such, the flexible timetable and carefully scheduled learning periods offered by business schools are especially convenient for busy female executives. In addition, many programmes are now offering special services to their participants such as concierge services, travel agency, child care and technical support.

Customised for you and your team

As an entrepreneur, small business owner or manager, you first need to ask yourself: what kind of programme are you looking for?

EMBA programmes, designed for candidates with over five years of work experience, focus on the business fundamentals (acquisition of a broad range of "hard" skills) as well as building soft skills that help transform managers into leaders. This combination, alongside the exposure to a classroom full of participants from different backgrounds, industries and job functions, gives the experience a powerful edge.

Consultancy projects (group assignments carried out to investigate a new project or venture for a company or to solve a problem) are a compulsory component of most EMBA programmes. Rachel Killian, MBA marketing and recruitment manager at Warwick Business School in the UK, explains:

> "At Warwick, most of your assignments can be work-based, so you really will be delivering value back to the organisation on a regular basis. You would also complete your consultancy project and dissertation on a topic that is of relevance and interest to your organisation; if they were to outsource this, it would likely cost more than your tuition."

General Management Programmes (GMPs) accommodate the more mature candidate with 10–15 years of work experience, and focus more on leadership skills, though many will also include an overview of business fundamentals. These courses tend to be shorter than EMBA programmes, and they range from just a few weeks of study delivered in seminar format to just under a year of study delivered in weekend or modular format.

The different topic-specific courses provided by business schools can range from strategy to leadership, marketing to finance, human resources management to pricing policies, digital media strategies to supply chain management. These open enrolment courses range in length from one to five days, and focus on the core matter of the subject area in question.

Winning results

Smaller enterprises can significantly benefit from executive education as it not only opens the mind to new ideas and ways of doing business, but it also creates a whole new circle for networking. Through fellow classmates, professors, campus staff, and programme alumni, the networking circle can reach numbers in the tens of thousands.

Scholarships and finance information

Executive MBA scholarships are becoming more innovative to help open up the EMBA classroom and attract more diversity among participants. Some of the scholarships on offer in Europe include the following.

- Ashridge: awards scholarships to candidates who have successfully applied to the Executive MBA programme and are in one of the following categories: women in leadership, emerging markets, responsible leadership, public sector, not-for-profit sector, armed forces leavers, post-redundancy/return-to-work.

- Cass Business School: offers scholarships for its Executive MBA programmes. Four "Dean's Scholarships", worth £10,000 each, are available for candidates in the Evening EMBA.

- ESCP Europe: one corporate scholarship for the European Executive MBA programme to SMEs to support them in the development of their talent and international expansion projects. The school also recently announced the creation of a new full scholarship fund for NGO professionals.

- IE: EMBA participants have access to scholarships and fellowships. The school also promotes or partners with leading financial institutions globally to facilitate the student loan process.

- IESE: the school's scholarship fund targets three different groups: women, entrepreneurs and candidates from emerging markets.

- INSEAD: five scholarships for its Global Executive MBA programme, dedicated to women, social entrepreneurs and candidates in active public service.

- London Business School: offers scholarships to outstanding candidates based in Dubai or the Middle East and women in senior management roles.

Entrepreneurs also have the opportunity to find funding with business clubs and incubators within the business school itself, often with the help of alumni or venture capitalists invited to the school or to chair business plan competitions. Check if the business school has a dedicated department or a research chair dedicated to entrepreneurship. Some business schools also conduct a significant amount of research on related subjects such as family-run businesses and innovation.

There are many fiscal advantages and tax deductions available for companies contracting with business schools and generally your accountant or even the business school advisers will help you in your learning and development project. In the UK, salary sacrifice schemes can be beneficial for both parties, employer and employee. Don't forget to contact your local Revenue & Customs department office to inquire about how salary sacrifice schemes can help with tax relief and reduce national insurance charges.

If you are sponsoring an employee, as a small business owner, you can attach some specific conditions to your employee's executive education project. These can include a contractual agreement to stay in the company for a certain number of years, a commitment to dedicating the consultancy project to a company-related need or sharing knowledge with co-workers via internal training sessions. Employers should also keep in mind that tuition fees can be negotiated in the case of "bulk" training sessions purchased or if you plan to send several employees back to school over a given period of time!

Hina Wadhwa-Gonfreville and Dawn Bournand are from Quacquarelli Symonds Ltd (QS), the world's leading network for top careers and education. Our mission is to enable motivated people to fulfil their potential, by fostering educational achievement, international mobility and career development. QS links graduate, MBA and executive communities around the globe with the world's leading business schools, universities and employers through a variety of platforms including websites, events, e-guides and technical solutions.

Responding to the needs of the market, the QS World Executive MBA Tour was launched in 2002 to help managers, executives and experienced professionals meet the world's top Executive MBA programmes in a relaxed and friendly environment.

For more information about the QS World Executive MBA Tour visit: www.topmba. com/emba.

View the QS Top Executive Guide: http://content.qs.com/teg/Top_Executive_ Guide_Spring_Summer_2011.html.

Website: www.qs.com.

PART 4
Access to innovation

N

NORWICH
UNIVERSITY
COLLEGE
OF THE ARTS

Work with tomorrow's creative talent today

if

Fresh talent providing:

- Brand consultancy
- Design consultancy
- Art commissions
- Media commissions
- Corporate art hire
- Apple iOS developer status

The Guardian Universities Guide 2011 rated NUCA as the best specialist Art and Design institution in England

The National Student Survey 2011 rated NUCA as the joint top specialist Art and Design institution in the UK

www.nuca.ac.uk/ideasfactory
ideasfactory@nuca.ac.uk
01603 610561

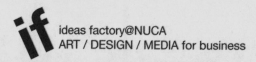

if ideas factory@NUCA
ART / DESIGN / MEDIA for business

17

Testing ideas

How to prove an idea and win the confidence of buyers

You have a great idea. But will it actually work? Will the market accept it? Will buyers be able to use it day to day? Most innovations stumble at one of these points. That is why so few make it beyond launch, let alone make a profit.

A typical source of failure is the discovery at a late stage that the specification you have developed is too costly, too impractical or too out of step with industry standards to go into production. You then order a re-design or downgrade your performance. You might save the day. But if you are struggling to engineer an idea at the right cost, then it might have been better to knock it on the head at an early stage.

As a start-up or spin-out, if a third party has proved your concept then you will inspire much greater confidence in buyers, who might otherwise see you as a crank inventor. In many markets, you will be expected to have taken your idea through a series of tests in any case. It has to work technically, of course, but will probably have to comply with regulations, such as health and safety.

In asking whether you are ready for market, you have to accept that you sit on a scale somewhere between a raw technology in which you have established the principles and an application that users are ready to buy.

Universities can be a valuable partner in moving you along this scale. They are independent and rigorous. They know their field and they are equipped to conduct experiments on your idea.

An unlikely inventor has used this route to take his idea to market. Simon Buckhaven is a barrister in his mid-sixties. On a holiday in France in the late 1990s, he was appalled at how lobsters were taken away and boiled, once you had ordered them from the menu. Surely there was a more humane, less barbaric method?

When he came home, he was astonished to find that no-one seemed to be giving any thought about stunning them like other livestock. So he set about developing his own more humane technique for crabs, crayfish and langoustines, as well as lobsters. He then filed a patent on his idea for an electrical stunner in a bath of briney water.

He knew he would only be taken seriously if independent experts in animal welfare had properly evaluated his idea. He tracked them down at Bristol University, where they were conducting a programme on fish welfare.

For £12,000 over 18 months, they tested Buckhaven's design using their own equipment. They confirmed that the shock was effectively instantaneous, then gave him the parameters for the most effective way of stunning these creatures.

Next, he went to the Silsoe Research Institute, a spin-out from the old Department of Environment, Food and Rural Affairs (DEFRA) to create the kit he would need for manufacture. After spending a further £10,000 over 18 months, he had two operating processes: one for producing a £2,500 version for use in restaurants and one at £50,000 for processing up to three tonnes an hour.

Both Bristol and Silsoe are highly regarded and professional, says Buckhaven. "The results have been crucial in opening up the market."

Branded the Crustastun and launched last autumn, Waitrose has already placed a number of orders for machines and is committing itself to the humane slaughter of crustaceans. Leading chefs such as Raymond Blanc are now adopting it in their restaurants and Prue Leith is using it in her cookery schools.

Two follow-up studies have further strengthened Buckhaven's case. One of the large seafood processors was conducting its own study with Glasgow University on why a reflex in crayfish and langoustines causes the meat to deteriorate so quickly. By using the Crustastun and eliminating stress, it found that you can retain the protein and taste for longer.

In another study commissioned by the Austrian government, Vienna University found that the Crustastun's electric shock created an interesting side effect. It also killed most of the bacteria on the creature as well. Instead of having to eat it immediately, you could keep it chilled for two to three days.

All of these are powerful features to make to the food industry, but Buckhaven has to satisfy an equally demanding audience: activists in animal welfare. One large charity in the US suggested he was paralysing crustaceans, rather than anaesthetising them.

To meet this charge, Buckhaven commissioned a £5,000 study from Glasgow University, which found that his technique did act as an anaesthetic on shellfish, leaving them brain dead. It also established that they were sentient. They could feel pain. It is a conclusion that challenges existing assumptions about how they are currently slaughtered and the results are being presented at the next global convention of the Humane Slaughter Association.

In running these kinds of tests and building a case, Buckhaven recommends writing a tight brief of what you want to achieve. "Otherwise you can find that your professor will start pursuing a sideline that suits his own research interests, not yours."

On his first series of tests with Bristol University, Buckhaven was able to piggyback onto a much larger project. On limited funds, you will have to wait for your results, however, if you have a larger budget, you can expect a significantly faster response than 18 months.

Buckhaven was always careful to tie up any intellectual property, making sure that he had the commercial rights in any outcome. By working through the commercial office at the university, he only once encountered any difficulty in reaching agreement on this basis.

When he started, Buckhaven had no intention of creating a small global business, but he is now following up interest in the US, Scandinavia, Australia and New Zealand. Once he scales up production, he will be looking to bring in more capital and find a production partner. The findings from his university tests will be central to any pitch he makes.

Tips for tests: Simon Buckhaven at Crustastun

- Find the leading expert in your field to evaluate your idea and test your assumptions.
- To keep costs down, see if you can piggyback onto any existing research.
- Make sure that you own the IP in any results.
- Track the results from research that buyers and regulators conduct on you.
- Understand the arguments that activists might use against you.

Feasibility studies

In developing an idea, a feasibility study is usually the first step to test the assumptions on which it rests and to explore its potential in new markets. Through Interface, a knowledge connection for business backed by the Scottish government, links and funds are being found for enterprises to run feasibility studies through universities. Recent projects include the following.

- A £5,000 grant to Cyberhawk to work with the UK Astronomy Centre to upgrade cameras on its unmanned aerial vehicles to improve its work in checking objects such as wind turbines and power lines.

- A project between Andrews, Bell & Christie, a firm of architects, and Robert Gordon University to investigate the degree to which Scottish housing associations can adopt low-carbon technologies.

- The University of Strathclyde conducted a report for Peacock Salt on the viability of its plan to create a low-carbon source of domestic sea salt in Scotland.

- A programme for AMT with Queen Margaret University to check the scope for extending its use of microwave technologies into the pasteurisation of fruit juice.

Funding to prove an idea

A new source of funding has emerged for smaller companies with ideas in science, engineering and technology. From April 2011, three types of grant became available from the Technology Strategy Board: up to £25,000 to prove a market; up to £100,000 to prove an idea; and up to £250,000 to create a prototype. This R&D scheme from the Technology Strategy Board replaces what the Regional Development Agencies used to offer.

Where next

www.crustastun.com
www.interfaceonline.org

18

Innovation labs

Universities are hosting innovation labs to release the dynamic within a group or a team

Office, lab, class or club? A new form of hybrid workspace is emerging to facilitate the rapid creation and capture of ideas. These innovation labs are designed to liberate the potential embedded within groups.

At spaces such as the Box at the London School of Economics and the Sandbox at the University of Central Lancashire, the goal is to use a wide range of creative techniques to speed up learning and to stimulate new patterns of thinking.

Innovating for value

Innovation is now more like a movie set. You bring together different specialists for a short burst of intense creativity. Then everyone disperses and moves onto the next project.

Few can afford the old linear model of innovation. Let someone think up an idea in isolation, then find a way of selling it. Markets are too open and moving too fast.

Instead, value is created in networks. As well as insights and perspectives from your designers and engineers, you want to know more upfront about where your market is heading, the state of the art in your industry, the potential for adopting techniques from elsewhere, what your users are expecting and how you can best scale up any ideas.

Almost inevitably, you will be asking yourself questions that cross boundaries and disciplines. Answers are just as likely to be found outside your organisation, as inside.

Innovation labs have emerged as a stimulating and rigorous means of capturing this multiplicity of views. On your own, you might form a consensus. In an innovation lab, you can explore.

Event space

Typically, innovation labs run for two to three days, although you might set up a series of events over a couple of months. At the Box and the Sandbox, groups as small as 20 and as large as 200 can be accommodated.

The spaces are deliberately designed to suspend your normal working environment. Instead, you will find yourself in a large, open, comfortable studio where the emphasis is on engaging your sense of curiosity and wonder. The idea is for you to explore, play and have fun. In that state of mind, you are much more likely to come at any task from a new angle.

Beneath this inviting stage, innovation labs are designed for hard creative work.

- To facilitate the emergence of fresh ideas from a complex environment.
- To accelerate learning across disciplines and geographies.
- To act as a crossover between academic and commercial disciplines.

A wealth of information

No-one understands a challenge better than those who are actively engaged in trying to solve it. Within any particular commercial context, there is a wealth of information in everyone's head and on the web.

The task of the support crew at an innovation lab, says Garrick Jones, a design fellow and innovation facilitator at the Royal College of Art and London School of Economics, is to capture all the information that participants generate in every format. Sound, video, documents, photographic. Then make this pool of knowledge instantly available to everyone else. These collaborative web tools let everyone navigate together through the cycle of creativity, design and production.

At the University of Central Lancashire, a "distiller" employs a technique for opening up questions on a screen to all the participants, who reply anonymously. You quickly start to build up a complex pattern of information.

At the Box, the approach is to appreciate this complexity in full, creating understanding from many different angles, before starting to allow a new order to emerge from the chaos that you have deliberately created. Like any natural phenomenon, there is a pattern or structure waiting to be found.

Learning solutions

A multi-modal approach is taken to exploring this knowledge, testing alternatives and considering decisions. You will be encouraged to embrace as many learning states as possible: visual, verbal, numerical, even musical.

You could find yourself making a model to express how you see an idea happening or how you see a change being made. Or you could create a scenario for an innovation, build a storyboard and shoot a video.

The purpose behind all this fun is to start putting ideas into action on the spot. The speed at which you learn and progress depends on how quickly facilitators can loop back your experiences to let everyone move to the next stage.

Where next

www.boxexchange.net
www.sandbox.uclan.ac.uk
www.ludicgroup.com

Sandpit for the oldies

In confronting a major public challenge, such as assisted living for the elderly, the Technology Strategy Board chose to start by bringing together ministries, researchers, corporates and enterprises in a "sandpit". All of them spent a week identifying the questions that really matter and looking at what could make a difference. How can we use technology to allow people to live longer in their homes, they asked? Unless we start to find some answers, then the social costs are going to be daunting. It is also potentially a big market in its own right. Once it has reviewed all the ideas that emerge from a sandpit, TSB then typically runs a competition looking for collaborative partners, whose funding it can match in bringing ideas to market.

Innovate the business model

If you are working for yourself in oil and gas in Aberdeen, then you may well rely on Freelance World for any accounting, tax and business support. Founded in 1999, the business has grown its turnover to £17m and has ambitious plans for growth.

After using traditional brainstorming techniques, it decided to try "design thinking" as a technique for visualising its current business model and generating future options for innovation.

The company's managing director, Alasdair McGill, admits not knowing what to expect from the two-day session at the centre for design and innovation at Robert Gordon University in Aberdeen. "We went into it with our eyes open, not really knowing what to expect. We'd heard of design thinking, but had never seen it in practice."

Under the direction of Julian Malins, professor of design at RGU, he was part of a cross-disciplinary team that created a model of how the business faces the market and how it delivers its service. By using a series of visual tools, they were encouraged to look at the business as a whole, challenge their own implicit assumptions and then re-phrase the questions they were asking themselves.

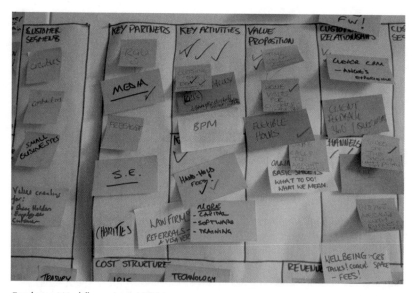

Freelance World's session at RGU

As a result of thinking like designers, they started to find gaps where they could improve and insights into how they could strengthen their appeal to freelancers across the UK and start working for micro-businesses in the creative industries.

The process that McGill and his colleagues followed blew them away. "No linear lists or left brain tasks. This was a very visual experience. Engage right brain! It made our heads hurt, but we got some real breakthroughs and an outcome that none of us could have foreseen."

19

Process improvements

Even arch-traditionalists can work with universities to bring their processes up to speed

The pace at which innovation now happens and the competition for business from the new economic powers in the East means that traditional industries are having to learn to adapt or throw in the towel.

Steel is a case in point. Fabricators in South Yorkshire may have a world-class reputation but they are no longer able to compete as bulk manufacturers. They have to find a way of specialising.

Users of steel in aviation, automotive and medical devices are actively looking for precisely engineered parts and for new alloys, using metals such as tungsten and nickel, as well as other material such as polymers. More than 50% of a commercial jet is now non-metallic, for instance.

To create a mechanism for matching this demand to the traditional skills in engineering in South Yorkshire, the University of Sheffield helped to create an Advanced Manufacturing Park (AMP) in partnership with Boeing and Rolls-Royce, which in the last decade has played an instrumental role in upgrading the supply bases in steel towns such as Sheffield and Rotherham.

It is a model to which the government is looking to create the big businesses of tomorrow. It is putting £200m into technology and innovation centres, which are designed to sit between universities and business.

As well as spreading knowledge and connecting businesses, they will give access to skills and equipment, which will allow suppliers such as Claro Precision Engineering to test ideas and build prototypes. Working with AMP, they made themselves more competitive by finding new feed and speed solutions.

By finding a competitive niche or adopting a smarter process, there is no reason why anyone who operates in a more mature area of the economy should not put themselves on an equally fast track to growth as other technology ventures.

Beyond tradition

Few companies occupied a more traditional niche than the Morgan Motor Company. Founded in 1909, it excelled in old-fashioned, hand-built sports cars, which sped you straight back to the classic days of motoring.

It began its journey towards a modern process for design in 2003. Without losing its distinctive reputation for craftsmanship, it wanted to adopt modern techniques and materials to improve efficiency and performance, as well as meeting the standards for breaking into the US market.

In a Knowledge Transfer Partnership (KTP) with Birmingham City University, a more modern approach to design was introduced that contributed to the aluminium structure, the automatic braking and the engine management in the model that was being developed to take Morgan into the US.

On the back of this transformative project, a second KTP was run with another graduate from Birmingham City to tackle manufacturing systems and production planning, which resulted in Morgan gaining an international standard for quality (ISO9001).

Against an original forecast for £150,000 in tangible benefits, the programme yielded £580,000 during its three years. A further £1.3m was expected in the following three years as a culture of continuous improvement spread from top to bottom of the company.

After putting in place the building blocks for a vehicle that conformed to all safety legislation and could be made more efficiently, the next goal to be pursued in another KTP with Birmingham City was to create a model that could appeal to a broader, younger audience without compromising Morgan's traditions.

In time for its centenary in 2009, a concept car was designed by Matt Humphries, who started as a graduate researcher at Morgan and is now its chief designer. Based on a positive reception from motoring critics, a limited edition of a hundred was planned. Priced at £110,000 each, all of the cars were pre-sold.

Further work has been undertaken with Birmingham City to create a modular platform for all Morgans, replacing the steel-ladder frame on the traditional chassis to reduce weight, improve handling and cut emissions. Morgan is also participating in an industry project to find alternative sources of power for its engine using hydrogen fuel cells.

Innovation at Morgan might once have been irregular and ad hoc. It might even have been resisted by die-hard enthusiasts. Thanks to the transfer of knowledge, techniques and skills from its university partner, the design process has become an integral part of its operations and creativity no longer depends on one individual.

Natural pioneer

For 30 years, Neal's Yard Remedies has been pioneering the use of organic and natural products for health and beauty. As a small company, its ideas can be restricted by resources, but it has extended its horizons through two projects with the University of Westminster, which were both run at a price it could afford.

First, it wanted to set up a good system for quality assurance, so it could manufacture in-house and launch new ranges more easily. The partnership with the University's School of Bioscience led to a serious reduction in its costs and sped up its times to market.

Two years later, it ran a second Knowledge Transfer Partnership with the school. This time, the task was to explore natural materials with inherent microbial properties so that it could replace all its synthetic preservatives with natural ones – a change that was fundamental to the image that the company was seeking to project.

It involved extensive research and screening of materials, which dramatically increased the expertise in formulation within Neal's Yard Remedies. In fact much of the knowledge on which it depends today in developing new products was gained through its partnership with Westminster. For the company, it has added value to its range and secured its position at the cutting edge of natural formulations.

Typical process improvements

- Move from fabricated assembly to design engineering.
- Create a culture of continuous improvements.
- Speed time to market for new products.
- Cut warranty claims.
- Meet international standards for quality and safety.

20

Buying in ideas

How to fast-track improvements into your business

As a small enterprise, it can be hard to think too far into the future. Your priority is the here and now. Close a deal. Keep a customer happy. Stick to your production schedules.

But to protect your margins and have a go at justifying a premium in the next year or so, you want to be sifting through ideas now for a new line or a new feature.

Your instinctive reaction might be to rely on generating your own ideas. After all, you know your market best and you can retain control of any investigation. On your own, however, your efforts can be patchy, expensive and inconclusive. Research is never easy or predictable.

Before you start ploughing in money to crack a challenge, it is worth taking a look at what ideas from outside you might be able to import. If you find the right one, you can take a short-cut through to innovation, saving yourself time and money. You might not even have to pay for the intellectual property that you are going to use.

This is the format in which innovations are now starting to work. More often than not, they are bundles of rights from different specialists on the value chain.

Venture capitalists are already picking up on the potential for this route to growth. In the past, they might have bought a technology venture, then bolted on some acquisitions, creating a sum greater than their parts, before making their exit. Now we are seeing a variant. Invest in a core technology, create a platform, then bring in new ideas on a revenue share. The upshot is that you now find technology executives speed dating on science parks up and down the country in the search for intellectual property that they can take to market.

In this market for ideas, universities are active participants, whose expectations have been refined by a decade of commercial experience. In the early 2000s, when many of today's technology transfer offices were created, it was hoped that universities could create steady streams of revenue by licensing their research. In reality, it has become clear that the bulk of any income comes from the occasional blockbuster. Many technologies tend to be too far from the market.

Universities now accept this reality and are ready to modify the terms on which they make technology available. Where possible, they will be looking to make a return, but in their role as a public body they also want to make sure their research makes an economic and social impact.

In a radical move, three universities, Glasgow, King's College London and Bristol, have created a new mechanism for engaging business. They are giving easy access to IP that is too early stage to justify conventional investment. Under a set of quick and simple agreements, business can adopt research outcomes for free.

The initiative represents a conscious signal to embrace a collaborative model for open innovation. Other universities are likely to follow.

As a small enterprise, you are unlikely to have the scale or capacity to take on technology that will change the game. One improvement, however, could be all it takes to make you stand out from the competition. How can you go about finding the right idea for you and then making the most of it?

Search and find

Contact between you and a university can happen in one of two ways. First, you may be approached by a university that is looking to license a technology into the market. Every year, they will be typically screening a hundred proposals for commercialising research. Ten might go forward. Two might spin out and the others will be licensed for commercial application.

Second, you can dig out opportunities yourself and build a landscape of the technology in your field of operations. Each university will publish a list of what it has available, although it can be hard to read for non-specialists. Or join a Knowledge Transfer Network that is relevant to you and start building up your contacts. Also take a look at the databases of intellectual property at the

Intellectual Property Office to gain a sense of who is taking a technological lead in your area.

More actively, you can write a spec of the challenge you are facing and circulate it among universities as a way of trawling for ideas.

Terms

Once you have found a candidate to adopt, you will want to ask yourself some questions about the basis on which you are going to use it. Is the intellectual property complete and in force, for example? How freely are you going to be able to use it and sell it as part of a package to anyone else? Can you sell it in all markets and through all channels? Are you going to have exclusive rights to the IP? Or will you share it with the university? Or with lots of other enterprises? Who pays if the IP is copied?

The university is likely to let you have a variation on its standard set of terms. Before taking professional advice, you can run some initial checks by reading through the licensing guidelines from the Intellectual Property Office.

What you pay

A sticking point with universities is that their expectations have been too high, expecting a payment upfront and a percentage of sales, when a technology may still be a long way from market.

Generally, you will now find an acceptance that research still has a long way to go to reach the market after it has left the lab. It might be worth talking to your partners about what other funding can be put in place to develop the idea.

Once it is ready to license commercially, you can discuss royalties, which can vary from a fraction of 1% to as much as 30%. One rule of thumb suggests that you should be paying 20%–30% of the total value the licence represents to you.

Particularly with smaller companies, many universities will be happy to adopt an open book in your negotiations. Share your commercial goals, set out your business model, give an estimate of your likely profit margin. Then the university is likely to accept a realistic figure. In a vacuum, they are almost bound to overprice it.

Know-how

IP is rarely a matter of supply and forget. It is only a snapshot of an idea at a point in time. The knowledge and intelligence continue. It almost always pays to find a way of building a relationship with the academics involved.

One option to consider is becoming involved in "translational" research, collaborating with academics in the early stages of a project to make sure that any outcome has a commercial dimension that can be licensed.

Full circle

The irony in buying in ideas is that you often develop innovations of your own based on how a technology is taken to the market. How do you design it, produce it, package it, use it and dispose of it? This surrounding knowledge can be highly valuable and open up new markets in its own right.

Where next

www.ipo.gov.uk/licensingbooklet.pdf

21

Contract research
When to ask a university to do your research

If you walk into a start-up or a national player in moisturisers and cleansers, you would probably expect to find at least a few white-coated scientists searching for wonder ingredients and creating fresh formulations for next season.

Actually, you might be surprised. Any direct manufacturing has long gone, of course, and research is now carried out under contract as well. Instead, these enterprises are largely run by brand managers who pick up signals from the market and turn them into ideas for new products.

For start-ups, the attitude is that you can find all the knowledge and skills you require to turn an original insight into commercial reality. Brilliant chemists are easy enough to track down. It is a matter of asking them the right questions and pointing them in the right direction.

Once you have made a name for yourself and are starting to challenge the market leaders, you can build up a wider set of relationships with different research teams. When you spot a trend emerging among your consumers, you just write a spec and put it out to tender.

It is more than likely you will end up working with a university, as they have the knowledge and facilities to run these kinds of projects. In 2008–09, these research activities represented a major chunk of their commercial operations, accounting for close to a third of all of the £3bn they earned from knowledge exchange.

Compared to other forms of collaboration, contract research is a more direct and straightforward transaction. It is usually employed to investigate and test ideas that are close to the market. You define the question to which you would like an answer and specify the outcome you are hoping to achieve.

Any results will belong to you. Under the templates produced by the Intellectual Property Office for how business can use university research, projects for creating new gels and soaps usually appear at the far end of the commercial spectrum. Under the IPO's fifth and final agreement, the IP resides with you and the university can only publish the results with your approval.

As a means of pursuing potentially lucrative new openings in the markets, contract research can be a highly flexible and effective tool for business. In 2008–09, the total value of such projects reached £937m, a 12% increase on the previous year.

For SMEs, whose resources and capacity for innovation are limited, it presents a chance to pursue questions they might otherwise have shelved. In 2008–09, their share of spending on contract research rose 4% to £38m.

It was this kind of specific challenge that Start-rite Shoes threw at the University of East Anglia. After launching its transactional website in 2008, it was doing well in offering parents a quick, convenient way to buy their children's shoes. But was there a better way of measuring feet at home?

To give sizes accurately time after time, you have to find a way of interpreting remote images taken from a variety of angles and distances, so any solution was going to take some original thinking from the consulting team at the university's school of computer science.

Their response was the Click 'n' Fit, a tool which lets you upload photos of your children's feet. Within seconds, you are given their size as accurately as if you were sitting in a shop.

The technically advanced image processing from the university is giving Start-rite the best measuring option currently available for measuring your feet at home, says Peter Lamble, managing director at the company. "Online shoppers are looking for ease and convenience without compromising quality. That is what we are giving them."

Further details on the model agreements for collaboration between business and universities can be found at www.ipo.gov.uk/lambert

Partnership Office, Faraday House, University of Salford,
The Crescent, Salford, M5 4WT
Tel: 0161 295 2902 · Fax: 0161 295 5494
Email: j.morana@salford.ac.uk
www.ktp.salford.ac.uk

Knowledge Transfer Partnerships

One of the University of Salford's most successful ways of working with industry is through the Knowledge Transfer Partnerships (KTP) scheme. KTP aims to help businesses to improve their competitiveness and productivity through the better use of knowledge, technology and skills that reside within the UK Knowledge Base. KTP is funded by the Technology Strategy Board along with the other government funding organisations.

With over 30 years of history, KTPs have evolved into one of the leading initiatives for engaging academic experts with innovating businesses. Projects can be undertaken in a wide range of areas including: product design, manufacturing, technical innovation, business processes (including IT and social sciences) and with businesses and organisations of all sizes in most industries and commercial sectors. Each KTP is part funded by a Government grant. The amount of grant is determined by the size of the company / organisation. A company with less than 250 employees can normally expect up to 67% grant, a large company or group can be entitled to up to 50% grant.

22

Research partnerships

As a partner, a university can broaden and deepen what you offer the market

Pick out your biggest challenge. Find the right academic for you. Agree a clear direction. Set up a joint programme for research. Fund it jointly. Turn it into a masters or PhD. Explore the process. Then look for any intellectual property to exploit.

It is a formula that has worked well for Hadley Industries in West Bromwich. Over the last decade, it has backed two doctorates and a master's, while upgrading its core operation as a roller of cold steel and creating its own technology centre. Sales have grown from £40m to £100m a year.

At the same time, Hadley has recognised that technology and IP create a new dimension to its business model. As standalone activities, they have opened up new routes to market and now account for a fifth of earnings.

Its technology centre has also given Hadley the breadth and scope to continue performing well during the downturn. The frames it used to make for use in building shopping centres may no longer be in demand, but it is now busy making tools to roll complex shapes for the licensees it has created through the IP in its research.

As a smaller company, have no fear in collaborating with universities, says Michael Castellucci, technical director at Hadley. "Here is a tremendous opportunity to give you background and breadth."

The main difficulty, he experienced, was in finding the right academic for the right project. "They tend to be specialists with their own focus. We found our current partner though our trade association. She was originally at Brunel University and we have followed her to Wolverhampton. It is all about the relationship. You have to be able to work well together."

The advantage in working with a university, he has found, is that you can focus on a big challenge outside the everyday distractions of customers asking questions. "You can be more blue sky in your approach," he says, "but you have to be clear about the direction you are taking. Draw up a clear agreement and be ready for any IP that results."

The cost of these programmes is met jointly by Hadley and by research grants raised through the university. Depending on the scope of the project, Castellucci expects his share to be in the region of £40,000 to £50,000.

On the IP, the university generally retains the background rights in the process that emerges from the research. Hadley has all the foreground rights that apply to rolling cold metal.

The first two doctorates that the company funded were to investigate further its original patented technology, Ultrasteel, which it had developed in response to a query from a customer. Its solution to dimple steel, as well as roll it, attracted interest around the world. Instead of setting up a new production line, Hadley started licensing its technology instead.

After experiencing the initial pleasure of earning revenues without making a capital investment, it realised that it had to keep investing to develop the technology. Two PhDs was the route that Castellucci and his colleagues chose to move forward.

In the latest research programme at Wolverhampton, they are looking at the role that knowledge management can play in engineering. How can you best model products and generate information more quickly for customers?

It may well not result in any IP, but the results will be directly applied within the business. As on the other research programmes it has run, Hadley will be looking to bring the PhD student it has funded into the technology centre.

As this programme comes to an end, Castellucci is looking at the next big question to explore in partnership with a university. As before, he will not be looking to develop a specific piece of intellectual property, but to open up opportunities for future growth.

Key points

- Find an academic in your field and make sure you can build a working relationship.

- Ask a big question, set a clear direction and explore the process, then see what IP you can exploit.

- Be ready for any IP that results and understand the difference between what happens in the commercial foreground and the academic background.

- Adapt your business model to recognise that IP and technology can become their own profit centre.

Me and the Giants

A new range of low-cost, high quality educational mobile games for young children has been launched under plans by a Glasgow-based company and the University of Glasgow.

The company teamed up with the institution to develop a range of games, designed for children between birth and 24 months, which will accommodate the different ways in which infants see the world, compared with their adult counterparts. A series of five games has been launched for the iPhone. Branded "Baby Look", they encourage the recognition of shape, colour and contrast, as well as the ability to distinguish between moods and emotions.

The company has been working closely with the University's department of psychology to ensure that the games will stimulate and educate children as well as entertain. Me and the Giants now plans to build on this relationship with the University by working with the faculty of education.

The collaboration was supported by the University's innovation network

Mobile games for children from Me and the Giants

programme, which aims to build links between the educational institution and Scottish SMEs. A £5,000 First Step Award enabled Dr Rob Jenkins, from the University's department of psychology, to work on the project.

For Will Adams, animator with Me and the Giants, the collaboration meant that the apps would educate, as well as entertain. "We are interested in stealth education. By working closing with Dr Jenkins, we have ensured the games stimulate and educate young children."

In the profit chair

Howden is a manufacturer of rotary twin-screw compressors, which are supplied globally for use in key industries including oil and gas. In 2008 as part of a major ongoing investment in product research, innovation and development at its Glasgow facility, Howden established a chair in engineering design and compressor technology at City University London to which Professor Ahmed Kovacevic was appointed.

In 2009, four major R&D projects were initiated to establish technology advantage by combining Howden's inherent know-how and manufacturing excellence with City's licensed intellectual property. The collaboration has given Howden the confidence to invest many times the national average of its revenue in R&D. In the last two years, its dedicated team has grown exponentially to include programmers and testers.

"We are using innovation to differentiate and expand our business reach," says the company's managing director, Jim Fairbairn. "Collaboration with City University London and particularly with Professor Kovacevic has contributed significantly to the management's ambitious strategy for growth in supplying products and services to major markets throughout the world."

23

Public research and competitions

How research grants are directed towards SMEs

Join a research consortium to free up cash and move yourself up a level? It sounds appealing, but unlikely. Surely grants for these programmes are too cumbersome for ventures in a hurry? If these publicly funded projects are about creating value in the long term, then is it just a case of leaving them to the major players?

Actually, no. At least, according to the funders of public research themselves. They are actively looking to recruit dynamic enterprises, because that is where innovation and growth most often lie. So targets are now being set for the participation of SMEs in major programmes and a series of smaller awards are being made for standalone projects.

In designing these packages, speed is a vital element for early-stage ventures, recognises Allyson Reed, director of strategy and communications at the Technology Strategy Board (TSB). "If made in the right way, such grants can be highly valuable."

All told, the TSB has 5,000 research projects under way and is running a competition a week on average. In size, they vary from £20,000 for feasibility studies to multi-million pound programmes. Over the last three years, there has been a definite shift towards mixing large-scale, multi-party projects with shorter, sharper challenges. For

Reed, the priority is simple: push into areas where there are roadblocks to the high-value economy of the future.

European programmes are looking to follow the same path of accelerating the development of high-growth ventures. Under the current Seventh Framework Programme (FP7), which is directing €54bn towards strategic research over seven years, a target of 15% has been set for SME participation. Similarly, the EU's joint technology initiatives in areas such as innovative medicines and clean skies are adopting frameworks for intellectual property that actively encourage the participation of SMEs alongside the major players and universities.

One spin-out that is relying on a grant to move beyond early stage is Molecular Solar, which emerged from the chemistry lab at the University of Warwick to commercialise its work in creating the next generation of solar technology. Its cells promise to be sufficiently light, flexible and affordable for use on portable electronic devices. Once adopted, a charger for a mobile phone, for instance, will roll up to the size of a pen.

That is still five years away. To fund the design of a ready-for-market application, Molecular Solar raised an initial £200,000 in seed capital on launch in December 2008 and subsequently won a £20,000 grant from the Technology Strategy Board to develop its materials. Earlier this year, it entered a competition for micro-solar technologies run by the TSB and the EPSRC (Engineering and Physical Sciences Research Council).

It was a tightly contested process, but it was part of a partnership that won a total package of £1.4m: £600,000 goes to the university to continue its research and Molecular Solar has £150,000 on which to draw in matched funds. Another £600,000 was awarded to three suppliers to make modifications which would not otherwise have happened. The rest of the money is funding further research at Imperial College.

As Molecular Solar spends its money on developing the cells, it can recover its expenses at a rate of 45% from the TSB. "For a spin-out like us, it is a highly effective way of leveraging scarce equity funding," says Peter Ballantine, the company's chief executive and veteran of two previous spin-outs that successfully scaled up, Bookham Technology and Southampton Photonics, now SPI Lasers.

The TSB's support is also giving credibility to Ballantine's plans to raise the next round of funding. Once the TSB project started, some additional equity was injected and Ballantine is aiming to raise a further £2.5m by the end of the year. Ultimately, the venture will require £5m to £10m to get off the ground, he believes.

"We are really pleased with the TSB grant," he says. "It is helping us bridge the gap and has created an ideal spin-out structure for us."

Another start-up that used research partnerships to fast-track its technology and accelerate its growth is Stingray. Some might have called its original ideas "pioneering". Others might have said they were "hairy".

Drawing on more than £1m in grants from the TSB, it is re-engineering the technique for identifying untapped oil reserves in partnership with the University of Southampton and two leading contractors to the oil industry. Instead of using conventional electronics, it adapted some fibre-optic sensors first designed for anti-submarine warfare.

"By putting together the right kind of grouping, you can build confidence and create global reach, which are always areas of major risk to early-stage ventures," says the TSB's Reed. For Stingray, it resulted in two early contracts from BP.

For those who are interested in collaborating on such research projects, the TSB has a facility, _connect, which will direct you towards a community of potential partners. "We want to draw on all the talent available," says Reed, "and direct entrepreneurs towards areas of interesting work."

Joint TSB/EU programmes

Four programmes are run through the Technology Strategy Board in partnership with the European Commission to support particular streams of innovation. Within each of these areas of strategic priority, funding has been matched for a diverse range of down-to-earth projects, including techniques for:

- removing lice from salmon in fish farms
- sending an automatic alert to make sure the elderly are up
- eliminating the greases, odours and smells from frying in restaurants
- operating remote-control vehicles under ice.

Two of these programmes are open to universities when working with an SME, as well as a European partner. Artemis is a £6m fund for embedded computer technology for any number of applications in areas such as automotive and aerospace. ENIAC is a smaller fund of £1.3m for embedded micro electronics.

The two other programmes are open to SMEs. Two calls a year are made for the £4m that Eurostars has for close-to-market innovations. Similarly, the £1.1m in Ambient is for business only. It is directed towards making it easier for the elderly to live independently. The focus of this year's call for tenders was mobility. Next year's priority is still to be resolved.

Finally, the TSB runs one-off initiatives with the European Commission, which appear under the banner of European Regional Area Networks, such as a recent, though now closed, fund of £5m for innovations to speed up web access.

All calls for projects appear on the competition page of the TSB's website, www.innovateuk.org/competitions.

EU research for SMEs

The EU runs the world's largest research programme, FP7, which actively seeks to involve SMEs as one of its goals. Officially known as the Seventh Framework Programme for Research & Technological Development, a total budget of €50.5bn is being deployed between 2007 and 2013 to build up Europe's capacity for creating new knowledge. SMEs are recognised as an integral part of the innovation system. The target is to channel 15% of all funds towards them.

As well as funding the search for new ideas and for cross-border collaborations, FP7 also has specific programmes for SMEs to outsource their research to external specialists, such as universities. The emphasis is on making an economic impact, so projects in all fields of science and technology are eligible. As a participating SME, you will end up owning the intellectual property in the results, which you will be expected to bring to market. For the EU, the goal is to improve competitive performance and to strengthen the link that universities have with smaller companies.

To qualify, you have to form a partnership of at least three different SMEs and two developers of research or technology. Projects last between one and two years with funding of between €500,000 and €1.5m. In 2010, 132 projects were funded at a total value of €136m.

"The scheme follows a bottom-up approach," says Steve Bradley at Beta Technology, who acts as the UK's national contact point on FP7. "Support is targeted at projects aimed at creating new knowledge or achieving results with a clear exploitation potential to improve or develop new products, processes or services which meet the needs of participating SMEs."

Further information about FP7UK can be found at: https://ktn.innovateuk. org/web/research-for-the-benefit-of-smes or www.betatechnology.co.uk

Business Development
Knowledge Exchange
Services to Business
Nurturing
Applied
Opportunity
Training
Testing
Engagement
Enterprise
Research
Catalysing Innovation and Knowledge Exchange
Leading Edge
Strategic Development
Commercialisation
Open Innovation
Knowledge Transfer Relationships Consultancy
State of the art Facilities Collaboration
Research Excellence
Innovation

The University of Huddersfield has a strong track record of working with companies across a variety of business sectors, including engineering, automotive, transport, chemical, biomedical, health, creative industries, digital and media.

These partnerships work in many different ways and we are keen to develop links with more businesses. We understand business needs and drivers and we believe that effective collaboration requires familiarity, trust and confidence. We can work with you to define your interests and identify opportunities for collaboration.

Services to Business
catalysing innovation and
knowledge exchange

T: 01484 473666
E: business@hud.ac.uk
W: www.hud.ac.uk/business

Enterprise and Innovation

The Enterprise and Innovation Centre (EIC), a £12 million flagship project due to open in May 2012, will be a landmark innovation project for the University and will signal a new approach to university-business engagement.

The facility, which is part-financed through the European Regional Development Fund and Kirklees Council, aims to establish a unique environment to support spin-in and spin-out companies linked to the University, to foster growth and economic regeneration within Huddersfield and the region. The Centre will bring together all the elements required for successful business growth under one roof – access to markets, finance, technology and skills, as well as traditional business support services.

The Centre will enable university researchers to engage directly with industry and maximise the impact of their research and development activities. It will also provide the infrastructure and resources to enable knowledge transfer and other collaborative project work between the University and external partners, fostering a new approach to open innovation within the university environment.

T: 01484 473666
E: business@hud.ac.uk
W: www.hud.ac.uk/business

University of
HUDDERSFIELD

Project Part-financed
by the European Union
European Regional
Development Fund
Investing in your future

Kirklees
COUNCIL

24

Technology and innovation centres

David Way at the Technology Strategy Board discusses a new force for innovation in the UK

The UK is not short of clusters and centres of scientific and technological excellence, from science parks to institutes in universities. All are evidence of the power of physical co-location; concentrating resources and expertise in one place, where people can work together and share resources, can be a powerful enabler of research and development excellence.

However, such centres and facilities have mainly grown piecemeal or through local efforts, whether by individual universities or businesses, or under the encouragement of regional authorities. What the UK has not had until now is a strategic approach to technology centres at a national level.

In recent years a major opportunity has become apparent: to create a world-leading network of centres, focusing on innovation in a few key areas of strategic importance to the future economic performance of the UK. Such centres would form a network with a common aim – to accelerate the translation and commercialisation of bright ideas into viable, marketable products and services.

As the technology entrepreneur Hermann Hauser highlighted in his 2010 report *The Current and Future Role of Technology and Innovation Centres in the UK*, many of the countries competing with the UK on the world stage already have such centres. In this country there is a gap in the landscape of resources available to accelerate the commercialisation of research. Sir James Dyson also highlighted this in his report *Ingenious Britain: Making the UK the leading high tech exporter in Europe.*

The opportunity is now being tackled head-on. In late 2010 the coalition government announced a major new commitment: the creation of a new network of technology and innovation centres with over £200m of government funding – a long-term investment in the future innovation capability of the UK. The new network would be established and overseen by the Technology Strategy Board.

The concept

The network of centres will be a transformational resource for UK innovation. Each will bring together the best of the UK's scientific and business expertise to focus on its own particular subject or theme, sitting between the worlds of academia and business, and enabling cutting-edge research to be translated swiftly into commercial opportunities. Creating a critical mass of innovation activity in their fields, the centres will reach into the knowledge base for world-leading technology and expertise, undertake collaborative research projects with business, carry out contracted research and enable businesses to benefit from technical expertise, infrastructure, skills and equipment that would otherwise be out of reach.

The centres will have the reputation to work closely with the best universities and other technology organisations in the UK and internationally. They will provide an innovative and entrepreneurial environment, enabling the development of new value chains and facilitating a variety of routes to the commercialisation of new products, processes and services.

The technology and innovation centres are being designed not to absorb or divert existing activities, but to make things happen which otherwise would not – generating a national scale of activity to benefit the entire sectors in which they operate, and beyond.

Establishing the network

The programme to develop the new centres moved rapidly. In January 2011 the Technology Strategy Board published a prospectus for the programme, and outlined the intention to create six centres between 2011 and 2013. The subject area of the first centre was also announced – in high value manufacturing.

Two further areas for new centres were announced in the first half of 2011 – cell therapy and offshore renewable energy. At the same time a further 10 potential candidate areas were identified, through a process of analysis and consultation with the research and business communities, as those with the most potential for a centre to have a catalytic effect in stimulating future economic growth. From these 10, three are being selected for further centres to be developed and launched by 2013.

For the investment in new centres to deliver its potential, this process of selecting the right areas is crucial. Combining the work of its own expert technologists with the views of the business and research communities, there are some key questions which have had to be answered in making these assessments. Is the sector or field one with massive potential for innovation and commercialisation? Does the UK have world-leading research capability in that field? Does UK business have the ability to exploit the technology and capture a significant market share? Will a centre attract and anchor the knowledge-intensive activities of globally mobile companies in the UK? Would this centre be closely aligned with, or even essential to achieve, national strategic technology objectives?

In summary, we have to ask: would creating a technology and innovation centre now in a particular field be the right solution at the right time, and add value beyond what already exists?

This process is not about winners and losers. The Technology Strategy Board emphasises that if the conclusion is that a technology and innovation centre is not the right intervention at the moment in a given field, there may still be huge potential in that area for other approaches and mechanisms to drive innovation in different ways.

The right shape for the right circumstance

The assessment process defines not only what focus the new centres will have, but also where they are to be established, by whom and what their shape will be; which may differ with the circumstances and conditions in each field.

In some areas there are already well-formed networks and communities, existing infrastructure, and investment and momentum on which to build. This was the case in High Value Manufacturing, where the centre was created from a consortium of seven specialist centres which either existed already or were in development, in locations ranging from Bristol to Glasgow – all leading-edge in their own fields of advanced manufacturing.

The cell therapy centre, on the other hand, is an example that is likely to be focused on one site. Other areas may have no obvious existing home, may be in their infancy, or may cut across sectors and disciplines and require new forms of collaboration. Again, these decisions are informed by working with business and other interested parties as the bids are developed, between the expression of interest stage and the final conclusion on how a centre will be established.

Working with technology and innovation centres

The technology and innovation centres will offer business a new model for working with the research community. The centres will have universities and research institutions as key elements – whether as part of their structure or working closely with them – giving business access to the expertise of researchers and scientists in a product-focused, entrepreneurial environment.

The centres will be designed to help small businesses as well as large, by encouraging collaboration and open innovation. The Technology Strategy Board's experience from its other research and development programmes is that collaboration is a powerful enabler of new developments; bringing together small companies and larger organisations which might not otherwise have met can pay unexpected dividends in terms of new ideas, relationships and supply chains, and physical co-location can enhance these benefits.

How will a company use a technology and innovation centre? Typically they would approach the business development person who would introduce the right people in the centre to start talking about specifics. One approach may be to explore what the client – the company – has and what the centre has, and put the two together to create something bigger and better. It might be that a business comes to use a piece of equipment they couldn't afford to buy themselves. They may find that there is another company in the centre with another piece of technology which, if combined with their own, could create something much stronger, or complete an offering for the market. The centre might work with business and academic partners to put together a collaborative R&D project, or might signpost the company to other competitions or sources of funding – but whatever the outcome, the centre will have provided the forum for meeting the companies and organisations who can help.

A new force for innovation

The new network of technology and innovation centres is a potent addition to the range of programmes and support available to accelerate innovation. With six new centres up and running by 2013, this is a long-term investment in the future economic capability of the UK which will benefit research and business alike; the expectation is that in coming years companies in a wide range of sectors and markets will come to see them as an invaluable resource in the development of their businesses.

David Way is Director of Knowledge Exchange and Special Projects at the Technology Strategy Board.

PART 5
Business models

Greenwich Research & Enterprise

UNIVERSITY
of
GREENWICH

Get the best for your business

At the University of Greenwich, our specialist facilities, expert training and world-leading expertise make us an exceptional place for business support.

Our team of business development managers are here to help you access all we have to offer:

- Business development
- Problem solving
- Consultancy
- Technology development

- Specialist equipment and facilities
- Access funding
- Training and development
- Student placements

- Staffing and support
- Knowledge Transfer Partnerships

Contact us today to find out how you can get the best for your business.

📞 +44 (0)20 8331 7867

@ enterprise@gre.ac.uk

🌐 www.gre.ac.uk/enterprise

25

IP commercialisation

License, spin-out or start-up? How to capture the potential in intellectual property

Intellectual property (IP) is a powerful but elusive asset. In itself, it is worth nothing. It only makes a return when you fit it into the right commercial format.

As one of the UK's pioneers of technology commercialisation said: "Enjoy the thrill of innovation, but remember to be hard headed about how you are going to commercialise any ideas. Most IP falls off an expensive cliff because it is so randomly managed."

In the last 15 years, Britain's universities have come a long way in developing processes for identifying and capitalising on research with commercial potential. In developing a strategy and finding a route to market, the choice revolves around how much autonomy is expected, attitudes to risk and the capital that is going to be required.

As a rule, any IP generally belongs to the university as an employer, but earnings are often split three ways between the academic team, their school and a central fund. Depending on the commercial route it chooses to take, the university can end up holding anything between 5% and 95% of the IP in a project. Essentially it will be looking at reaching the market by way of three main channels:

1. licensing

2. spin-outs

3. start-ups.

As a back stop, it could just sell the IP. We are now operating in a much more active market for ideas. Major players accept that innovations are just as likely to be created outside the organisation as inside. IP can be either auctioned or traded.

As a piece of raw technology, it is hard to put a value on any IP. Yes, you can look at the economic cost of developing it, but it is hard to make an estimate based on its future impact on earnings.

If you are going to sell it at anything much over cost, you have to build in as much value as you can in the form of lab books, prototypes, working models, proofs of principle and approvals. Even so, the danger remains that you could be letting a promising technology go too cheaply. For universities, the challenge lies in identifying potential winners and working out how far they are prepared to go in developing an idea for profit.

Licensing

If capital is tight and risks are high, licensing can give you the most direct route to growth. You wrap up the IP in one of your ideas and pass the rights to a commercial partner. Without much upfront cost, you can find yourself in markets that you might otherwise have struggled to reach.

Your licensee will take responsibility for setting up production and marketing. In return, you earn a percentage on each sale they make in the form of royalties. Depending on the strength of your IP, you might ask for a down payment. You might even negotiate a consultancy fee for passing over your knowledge of how the process works.

As well as letting you roll out winners at speed, licensing gives you a mechanism for exploiting minor improvements, entering secondary markets and seizing brief moments of opportunity. The chip designer, ARM, grew from the Cambridge Science Park by building its whole business model round adapting and licensing its technology to the world's producers of microprocessors.

To reach a position where the cash is flowing, you have to find the right partner. Size is one consideration, but an enthusiasm for your technology counts just as much. Like any relationship, it can be easy to start, but difficult to end.

Questions that you want to resolve at the beginning rather than dispute later include the following.

- The scope of your IP: can you offer a complete package? Do you have to ask anyone else's permission?

- The degree of exclusivity: is your licensee the only one who you can use your IP? Can you both use it? Or, like ARM, are you going to talk to all the players in the market?

- Are you going to restrict your licence to a particular purpose or to a particular market?

- Who has the right to follow up any improvements?

- How long is the agreement going to last? Can you bring it to an end if performance is below expectations? Could there be a penalty if targets are missed?

- If the project does well, your IP will almost certainly be tested by someone. Who is going to be responsible for taking action?

Depending on the terms that you agree, royalties can vary from less than 1% up to 30%. One rule of thumb is to calculate the total value that your IP represents to a licensee. Then ask for a 20%–30% share.

Licensing specialists such as Christi Mitchell at Highbury know which benchmarks to expect. In software, royalties will be low, based on non-exclusive agreements negotiated within hours. In life sciences, terms can take months to settle and rates revolve round 5% for a worldwide exclusive to justify the upfront investment. In engineering, which is a more recent convert to the licensing model, there is more freedom to negotiate terms.

Timing can be significant in setting a value as well. If you are too early, there may be too many unknowns. If you are too late, then the market might have already moved beyond your idea. Probably the best time to start talking to licensees is when your IP first enters the system.

Spin-outs

For exciting, unproven technologies, spin-outs create an alternative route for reaching the market. Knowledge and assets are transferred into a new, independent business, which raises early-stage capital to give itself the freedom to turn research into a product that will sell. Once the spin-out establishes itself and starts making profits, its investors can make a return through a trade sale or a flotation.

Success can come from unexpected lines of inquiry. One group of geologists spent 20 years developing a technique to measure the magma in volcanic chambers. Once it was realised that it could be adapted in the search for oil and gas, a company was created and floated on AIM. On its share of the proceeds, the university's school of geology was able to buy a ship to conduct further studies in oceanography.

Spin-outs tend to be used in the following situations.

- You are developing a disruptive technology that major players are unwilling to accept as yet.

- You have the chance of creating a platform technology which everyone in the industry will have to buy.

- You are creating a technology that can only be developed with funds from outside the university.

- You have to consolidate the IP from a number of universities and institutions to move it forward commercially.

Clearly, the risks of failure in such enterprises are high. In some cases, the university may decide to play a relatively passive role and transfer the assets to a management team. More probably, it will play an active role in preparing the commercial case. At research universities, for instance, 100 candidates a year might be screened, 20 taken forward and then two or three turned into spin-outs.

From the start, the spin-outs must clearly own all the IP they need. If doubts are raised later, it can be ruinous.

IP is a snapshot of how a technology stands at a moment in time. The knowledge behind it will continue to develop. Most spin-outs like to gain the rights over any research that the university subsequently conducts in their particular field. Realistically, the benefit usually only lasts two to three years, before academics start pursuing other lines of interest.

One lesson from the US is that spin-outs do well when academics are actively involved in transferring their knowledge to those charged with turning science into engineering. As one innovation director at a spin-out said: "We want to fail fast, not learn slow."

However, spin-outs will have to decide how close they remain to the university. By being separate, no questions arise about who actually owns any IP and they are free to drive forward the business. Executives expect to make decisions at a different speed from scientists.

Similarly, care has to be taken in designing the capital structure of the spin-out. As well as equity for the scientific founders, the university will expect a significant stake in return for its IP. More questions arise about how much will go to the executive team who are going to drive forward the business. Generally, spin-outs work best when they find a balance between technological creativity and entrepreneurial drive.

In spin-outs, the risks are typically different from other start-ups. As academics, the founders will have years of technical experience, so the challenge is less proving whether a technology can work and more in converting it into something that anyone would want to buy. Generally, universities recognise that it is best to let academics focus on their own areas of expertise and to bring in executives to run the business. Why let a research scientist leave and have a go at running a business?

Since 2008, the appetite for flotations on markets such as AIM has collapsed. Early-stage investors, however, are still active and tend to fall in one of two camps. Those who back technologies that have squared off most of the risks and are close to market; and those who are still prepared to take a calculated chance on technologies that could go global.

Start-ups

Universities have always been a springboard for start-ups. Students pursue ideas that they have tested in their studies and academics set up their own consultancies. Now a new generation of academic entrepreneurs is operating in the space between the university and the market.

Often the university has no claim on the IP that is developed or the idea is too small to justify putting in its own resources. Rather than let it go, as happened in the past, universities are looking to host the growth of these business ideas.

At incubators such as Innospace at Manchester Metropolitan University, start-ups are offered low-cost space supported by advice on planning and by training in business skills. For students and graduates, it creates a practical platform for bringing ideas to fruition. For the university, it strengthens its position as a place to start and grow a business.

Find the right path to market

The Intellectual Property Office has produced an online tool that is designed to help anyone with an idea to put their commercial thoughts in order. It is designed for those who already understand the technical aspects of their IP, but are looking for guidance on how to turn it into a business plan.

You are asked a series of stage questions. After checking the status of your IP, it explores your options for exploiting these rights. Are you going to use your own resources to build a business? Do you need a partner to capture the full potential of your idea? Or does it make sense to sell a licence and earn a stream of royalties?

In each case, you are taken down a logical path. Questions are strategic at first. In which markets do you want to be? What skills do you need? Do you have the cash to make it happen? What happens if anything goes wrong? How quickly are competitors going to respond?

You will then be asked a series of more specific questions about your IP. If you are going to do a deal, who will end up owning the IP and who has the rights to any follow-ups? What happens when someone challenges you? How do you divide up the money?

The idea is that you can test a series of scenarios, before you start talking to anyone more formally. Published under the title "Licensing your IP", the tool involves 20–25 questions and takes about an hour to complete.

Where next

www.les-bi.org
www.ipo.gov.uk/iphealthcheck

26

Innovation value

How to bring an innovation closer to market

Too often, the ideas and knowledge that emerge from universities fail not because of any technical shortcomings, but because the market is approached from the wrong angle.

You might have a platform technology for which everybody is waiting. Then by all means, build a business round a master patent. But IP rarely sells itself.

As an innovator, you have to prove your value to the market. Time and again, creative efforts are directed towards perfecting an idea and too little time is spent asking three questions that determine whether you are likely to make any kind of return or just join the 90% of innovations that fail.

1. How close in reality are our ideas to market?
2. What value might our customers actually place on what we offer?
3. What is the optimum approach for generating revenue?

In the early stages of developing an idea, you have to be discreet in what you say. But there is an equal risk in launching yourself on an unsuspecting world. You cannot just rely on being better. You have to understand where you add value for your customers.

Even then, you can make no assumptions about where the money is going to be made. It is easy to think you can just adopt your usual channel to market and use the same pricing structure as your competitors. In fact, it is a feature of high-growth enterprises that they take apart any conventions and find a business model to maximise their revenues.

As Allyson Reed, director of enterprise and communications at the Technology Strategy Board, argues:

> *"Innovation only really starts when you take it to market. Will it work commercially? Is it at the right price point? Is the market ready? You have to be focused on how you are going to compete. That can mean wrapping a service round a product and developing a new business model. You have to see the technology in context.*
>
> *It is tough trying to find the right application. In voicing the market need, you have to stay open to a different range of solutions and realise you might have to bring in technologies from outside. Do not be fooled into thinking that you are closer to the market than you really are."*

Close to market

In an industry such as food, you see two types of innovation. The search for the next wonder ingredient sits alongside the surrounding know-how of how a product is made, packaged, used and recycled. The value can lie at any point in this chain.

To appear on the shelves, it is almost inevitable you will have to buy in technology from other partners. You might be sitting on a breakthrough, but you have to be realistic about how close you are to market. A radical technology takes years to develop. You can stake everything on it, but you run the risk of creating a single point of failure.

Instead, it can be better to find a series of specific applications, then form partnerships in which everyone understands the different roles they are playing in the creation of value. Of course, you will want to protect your intellectual property, but you want to be in a position to use it as flexibly as you can.

Talk to the market

You also increase your risk of failure by pursuing an idea in isolation. The fear is that you will alert your competitors to what you are doing. But without early-stage marketing, you will struggle to turn invention into revenue.

In the experience of one specialist in technology commercialisation, Peter White at YTKO in Cambridge, there is no need to discuss the particular features of a technology that you are developing. But you can talk about the direction you are taking and the benefits you are aiming to offer.

By engaging potential customers right from the start, you will understand more about the problems they would like you to solve and the actual value they place on you being faster or better. You are almost certain to find some unexpected angles.

At these early stages, you can keep it experimental and informal, but you will be well down the line to creating a proposition based on what the market wants. Later, once you start discussing your technology in detail, you can start operating under confidentiality. By then, you have set the scene and have gained an insight into what you might be able to charge.

The approach you take

Once you know where the value lies in an idea, it pays to have an open mind about how you are going to approach the market and maximise your revenues.

- Are you just going to sell your product? Or could you offer follow-ups? It is a model widely adopted for razors, desktop printers and aircraft maintenance. A clever piece of technology is sold at close to cost. The profits are then made on refills and service.

- Or could you bundle your idea up as a financial package? A technique for detecting eye problems would normally cost £150,000 upfront. Instead, clinicians are offered a three-year contract based on a monthly charge for the patients they see. This arrangement overcomes any reservations about the capital cost, as well as creating a recurring stream of revenue.

- If you have developed a new technology, could you offer to run the whole process for your customers, instead of just supplying the equipment?

- Alternatively, could you just supply them with the know-how, while you focus on developing the underlying technology? As a model, it can be a highly lucrative, low-cost route to growth.

- Do you have any scope for challenging the assumptions under which your industry operates? Until the Nintendo Wii, for instance, computer games were dominated by high-speed action driven by faster processing and evermore realistic graphics. By re-packaging the technology to appeal to families and to groups, Nintendo opened up a completely new segment of the market.

There is no right way of designing a business model. You just have to be alive to all the potential lines of revenue, be ready to challenge assumptions about your market, design a powerful value proposition and put in place a capability to match it.

27

Grant funding

The types of grants available to businesses and how to go about accessing them

As a smaller company, you are likely to focus on one innovative project at a time. At a university, the knowledge transfer office will be working on dozens each year, so will have a good grasp of how you might set up grants to support what you are doing.

Usually, you will be expected to match any funds. Sometimes you might be given a full grant. Either way, you have a number of options for offsetting the costs in developing your ideas and bringing them to market.

Knowledge transfer

In working with universities to find new solutions and make improvements, Knowledge Transfer Partnerships (KTPs) are the flagship programme for bringing in the best minds to your company. Typically, a graduate will come and work for you under a senior academic's supervision for one to three years. A new product, a new service or a new process might be the result.

Two-thirds of the cost is met through a grant from the Technology Strategy Board in recognition of the value that is created for the university in undertaking these kinds of collaborative project. As an SME, you pay for the rest, although you have the chance to review your involvement after three months.

"KTPs are a great way for an SME to access expertise that they otherwise could not afford," says Dr Carol David Daniel, head of technology transfer at City University London. "Universities value the opportunity to engage in them as much as small businesses. For academics it is an excellent chance to ensure that their research is relevant and active."

The scheme has been running for over 30 years and typically funds well over a thousand projects each year. All forms of commercial activity are included.

The calculation is that the cost for an SME is significantly lower than recruiting a new member of staff directly. As well as bringing in a researcher into the business to work on a problem for you, you gain access to the university's knowledge in your field as a whole under the supervision of a senior academic.

For SMEs, there is an option to run shorter programmes of between 10 and 40 weeks. After a recent confirmation that the scheme will continue as an integral part of the government's commitment to accelerating innovation, SMEs can also qualify to pay 25% instead of 33% of the cost.

Other programmes can be run directly through the UK's seven Research Councils. Although their primary role is to fund the work of academics, they also run schemes to fund the placement of students and academics within your company.

All Research Councils offer CASE studentships (Collaborative Awards in Science and Engineering), for instance, which support research for doctorates being carried out in collaboration with a business partner. In return for setting the direction of the research, you will typically be expected as a partner to cover a third of the costs, which can total £70,000 over three years.

First steps

In Scotland, Wales and Northern Ireland, official schemes to encourage local SMEs to engage with universities run under the title of "innovation vouchers". Channelled through your academic partner, you are given a credit for running a research or consultancy assignment with the university. The schemes are designed to encourage collaborations that might not otherwise happen. Normally, you are expected to cover half the costs.

In England, such schemes disappeared with the demise of the regional development agencies. However, many universities are running their own versions to encourage SMEs who are thinking about setting up an engagement for the first time. Newcastle ran its own credit scheme for £5,000 over six months which resulted in 125 new relationships with SMEs.

Aston has just won an award from *The Times Higher Education Supplement* for the well-established voucher scheme it manages for a number of universities in the West Midlands. Through seven rounds of funding, 670 local SMEs have run projects with universities. Without the voucher, it is unlikely that many of them would ever have become involved.

Testing ideas

A fresh source of funding has emerged for smaller companies with ideas in science, engineering and technology. From April 2011, three types of grant became available from the Technology Strategy Board: up to £25,000 to prove a market; up to £100,000 to prove an idea; and up to £250,000 to create a prototype.

This R&D scheme from the Technology Strategy Board replaces what the regional development agencies used to offer. The scheme will run alongside existing programmes in Scotland, Wales and Northern Ireland.

Under proof of market, you can research a market, analyse competitors, develop your intellectual property and start planning your commercialisation. Such projects to assess your commercial viability can last nine months. The most you will be awarded is £25,000 and you will expected to cover at least 40% of the cost.

In exploring whether your concept is technically and commercially feasible, you can apply for £100,000 over 18 months. Again, you will be awarded a maximum of 60% of your costs.

Finally, in developing a prototype, which includes demonstrators, testing and intellectual property, grants of £250,000 are available over two years. If you are small, then up to 45% of your costs can be funded. If you are medium-sized, the upper limit is 35%.

Strategic programmes

To develop key technologies or meet challenges in public policy, government bodies run competitions to find potential partners and match their funding in finding solutions. Priorities are identified under the auspices of the Technology Strategy Board (TSB), which draws together a programme in partnership with all the main players in the market. It then launches an open competition to search for potential partners, who are almost always expected to work in collaboration.

To accelerate the creation and adoption of ideas, the TSB recognises that it is better to pool knowledge and co-operate in networks of value, so it actively encourages the involvement of SMEs, whose focus and adaptability often puts them ahead of the game.

Under the Small Business Research Initiative, the TSB enables SMEs to bid to develop innovations for challenges identified in the public sector. If accepted, you are typically awarded up to £100,000 to prove within six months whether your idea is technically feasible. The most promising candidates might then receive £1m over two years to run demonstrations.

Even in the EU's flagship programme for building up cross-border research, Seventh Framework Programme, which is running a €50bn programme over seven years, recognition is given to the ingenuity and creativity of SMEs. A target has been set of directing 15% of those funds towards them. More details can be found through the TSB or through knowledge transfer offices.

Specialist sources

Like the government, a number of other, more specialist bodies will have an interest in those who are developing solutions in their area of operation.

In health, charities such as the Wellcome Trust, which has invested £100m in turning research into products, and the National Institute for Health Research, which awards grants of up to £100,000 to test the viability for early-stage collaborations, can be instrumental in taking an innovation forward.

Similarly, in clean tech, the Carbon Trust is doubling the size of the grants available under its flagship Applied Research Scheme from £250,000 to £500,000. Other bodies, such as the Waste and Resources Action Programme, also run their own innovation funds.

R&D tax credits

The main incentive that the government offers for business R&D is through a tax credit. The relief on qualifying expenditure in April 2011 rose from 175% to 200%. Next year, it is going up to 225%.

Many early-stage enterprises are not in profit, of course. For them the unusual attraction of the scheme is that instead of carrying forward their losses to set against future profits, they can claim a cash payment now on 25% of qualifying expenditure.

In 2008–09, 8,350 companies claimed a total of £980m under the scheme. About 80% of them were SMEs.

Michael Stean, tax partner at Baker Tilly says:

"It is a good concept. In the early years, instead of x amount in losses, you have y amount in cash. The difficulty lies in the detail. Expenditure qualifies, but capital doesn't. Then will the government accept what you are doing as genuinely innovative? All the same, it is a useful top-up. SMEs are always starved of cash and never starved of losses."

Lean business models

In the downturn, a number of enterprises have found ways of creating their own lean business models by pulling together a funding package for their innovation drawing on all these kinds of support packages. They have even traded their IP to gain access to research facilities at universities and corporations. So instead of going down the traditional route of asking for hundreds of thousands in equity upfront, they have found that a small, close-to-virtual team can take an idea a long way beyond proof of concept and proof of market.

Where next

www.innovateuk.org
www.scottish-enterprise.com
www.business.wales.gov..uk
www.niinvest.com
www.carbontrust.co.uk/emerging-technologies
www.wrap.org.uk
www.wellcome.ac.uk/Funding/Technology-transfer
www.ccf.nihr.ac.uk

The seven UK Research Councils

1. Biotechnology and Biological Sciences Research Council

2. Economic and Social Research Council

3. Engineering and Physical Sciences Research Council

4. Medical Research Council

5. Natural Environment Research Council

6. Science and Technologies Facilities Council

7. Arts and Humanities Research Council

28

Locate on-site

The benefits of locating a business within a university's innovation or enterprise centre

The space between a university and the market can be an attractive base for a spin-out or for your own start-up. Within an innovation or enterprise centre, you can operate on flexible terms until you are ready to grow. You can keep yourself up to speed with the latest thinking in your field. You can bring in specialists. You can use state-of-the-art facilities to test your ideas. You can join a cluster of like-minded enterprises. You can call on business advice and support. You can put yourself in front of investors within the university's network.

At some universities, such as Coventry, which occupies a 60-acre site in the middle of the city on the old Rolls-Royce plant, you can move from early stage to full operation without leaving the campus. At others, facilities are more spread out, but can still put you on an escalator to growth.

The experience is quite different from a serviced office, says Margaret Henry at Oxford Innovation, which accommodates 500 enterprises in 20 different centres across the country. "They are meant to be about collaboration and growth, encouraging you to make contacts and raise finance. We are deliberately looking to foster a community of entrepreneurs."

Virtual tenants and hot desking

To get you started and to test the water, you can adopt a virtual presence in an innovation centre or technology park. For about £100 a month, you will be given an address, someone will answer your calls, you will be able to drop into the centre, you can hold a meeting, you can book a room and you will be invited to networking events. For perhaps £200, you will be able to use a desk for a few days a month.

Incubators and innovation centres

Incubators tend to operate within the university. Innovation centres are run outside. Both offer space and support on flexible terms. Rather than committing to a lease for a number of years, you take out a licence month by month. It is easy to scale back, if your idea fails to meet expectations, or move upstairs into a bigger office when you pick up speed.

What might an incubator look like? At the University of Manchester, there are now five. The first, opened in 1999 next to the Faculty of Medicine and Life Science, is for bio-tech ventures. "It is designed as a space where you can circulate and meet," says Tony Walker at the University's incubator centre, "and where you can use test equipment which would otherwise be prohibitively expensive."

The rent at such centres tends to be just above the local commercial rate, because so many extra growth services come as part of the package. You will be able to ask questions of a business adviser, for instance. Oxford Innovation might also find you a coach and help put together your senior team.

Enterprise centres and grow-on space

Currently, 60% of the occupants at Manchester's bio-tech incubator are university spin-outs and 40% are external ventures. Once they have proved they have a market, they can move into a grow-on space within the "health corridor" that the University is creating. "It is just opposite the teaching hospital," says Walker, "so they are well placed to start conducting clinical trials."

On the campus at Coventry, you can move into similar enterprise centres, depending on the industry in which you operate. For product designers, there is a specialist hub, which houses Tata Technologies, part of the group that now owns Jaguar Land Rover, as well as part of the faculty. Or there are similar institutes in areas such as health, computer games, creative industries and construction, which operate as a halfway house between research and industry.

Business and science parks

Once an enterprise starts to become operational, it will want to fit out its own space and have the security of a lease well into the future. At Coventry, you can stay on campus and move into the Innovation Village, which offers a choice within eight large buildings.

At Manchester, the next natural step is the science park, which is part-owned by the University. Over the last 25 years, it has grown into eight purpose-built buildings, which house over a thousand people in all areas of economic activity.

"We want to grow and retain the knowledge base," says Tony Walker. "Across all our spaces for innovation, we have a revolving door, creating room for growth for smaller companies who want to collaborate with the University."

29

Venture funding

The different sources of investment finance available to university-based ventures

The latest spin-out from the University of Oxford has two unusual features. First, it comes from a doctor of ancient Greek in the classics department. Second, it is funded by a Chinese angel investor.

The launch of a handheld scanner in September 2011 to read faded or hidden writing on ancient manuscripts reflects how far knowledge transfer offices are now reaching to unearth promising ideas and to find the funding to support them.

Ten years ago, they were sticking to a more conventional script. Ideas from academics in the software, life sciences and engineering were backed by investors within half an hour's drive. Now a much wider creative and financial net is being cast.

"You never know where the exciting ideas are going to come from," says Tom Hockaday, chief executive of Isis Innovation, the company that was created to commercialise technology from Oxford in 1987 and that has just spun out Oxford Multi Spectral from the department of classics. "We have the enthusiastic researchers and the protectable pieces of science. We are missing the money and the management."

He sees his role in assembling the team and keeping it together. "It has always been a three-dimensional challenge. We connect the world of research with the world of commerce and the world of finance. Now we have a fourth dimension, as investments start to come in from China, Hong Kong and the Middle East."

Not all universities can draw on the reputation or resources of Oxford, but they are still exploring all the options that are available to them. Coventry, for instance, runs an equity committee, on which entrepreneurs, investors and bankers sit alongside the vice-chancellor and the University's director for enterprise. Together they screen any ideas that are coming through the University with a view to plugging them into funding networks within the West Midlands.

To find the backing for such early-stage ventures is never easy. The risks are too high for bank finance, of course, and conventional venture capital generally prefer ideas that have already reached the market. Unless they fall for a fad or jump on a bandwagon, investors are wary about committing to technologies that they do not understand. The paradox is that real wealth is created from those innovations at the cutting edge that re-shape the way the world works.

The £250,000 invested in Oxford's multispectral imager looks a promising candidate for making a return. It has already been used to restore over a quarter of a million historically significant manuscripts and could also find a secondary market in detecting forged security documents. In raising the funds to bring such ideas to markets, universities have a series of options which they can bring into play.

Seed capital

To prove a concept or build a demonstrator, universities often invest amounts of £5,000 to £25,000 from funds that they manage themselves. The University of Manchester, for instance, has a £3.2m line of finance to help it jump through the main hurdle in technology transfer: to develop a prototype with a robust proprietary position and a credible strategy.

"We like to have ready-to-hand funding for proof of principle and proof of market to meet our deal flow projections," says Clive Rowland, chief executive of UMI, the University's innovation group. "We can then get projects launched which would otherwise not see the light of day."

Similarly, Oxford has two funds for testing inventions and Coventry now has a facility through the Higher Education Innovation Fund to put £5,000 into proof of concept.

Spin-out capital

Once verified, an idea is now in a much better position to attract larger amounts of money. The conventional route is to raise £500,000 from private investors, or angels as they are commonly known, before approaching venture capitalists for subsequent rounds of £2m, then £5m.

On average, spin-outs from Oxford are currently raising £850,000 in the first round. "It is a chunky amount," says Tom Hockaday, "but technology needs a lot of investment to create value and move it closer to market."

The main forum for raising this money is through the Isis Angel Network, when a room of up to 150 potential investors gathers to screen four or five proposals. Typically, they used to be local entrepreneurs who had sold their own ventures and were ready to put their funds and expertise back into early stage ventures. Now they are a much wider mix. Together with high net worth individuals from China, private equity is represented within the network as well.

Sometimes, one investor will take the lead and pull together a consortium. Or Isis will pull together a group of between three and 20 individuals. Sometimes, as in the case of ancient manuscripts and Oxford Multi Spectral, Hockaday and his colleagues will be approached by an intermediary on behalf of an international investor.

The angel market

Such angel networks are usually managed by companies such as Oxford Investment Opportunity Network. Operating on a national basis, its main network raises investments of between £100,000 and £2m. For angels, who are interested in higher risk at the early stage, it runs a network for concept funding of between £25,000 and £100,000. In the last three years, Oxford Investment Opportunity Network has raised a total of £27m in direct investments from angels for 40 different ventures.

Such support for innovative ventures is about to be strengthened by the government's new co-investment fund. Once a venture has a commitment from its angels, it can draw down a similar amount, so doubling the size of the funds it has raised. A similar scheme runs in Scotland (the Scottish Co-Investment Fund).

"It is designed to leverage money from angels," says Margaret Henry at Oxford Investment Opportunity Network, which is one of the five syndicates of early investors who will be putting forward deals to the managers of the £50m fund, Capital for Enterprise. "It is a pot to invest alongside the private sector, rather than giving out subsidies through grants."

The co-investment fund is for any venture, not just those associated with a university. It will run on a national basis and is expected to launch in late 2011 as part of the government's £450m regional growth fund.

Capital for Enterprise is a limited company governed by an independent board with the Secretary of State for Business as its shareholder. It has been established to be the government's principal source of knowledge, expertise and information on the design, implementation and management of finance measures to support SMEs. It has become the largest single investor in UK early-stage venture capital and manages investments of more than £550m in around 40 venture funds.

As well as Oxford Investment Opportunity Network, the other organisations participating in the fund alongside Capital for Enterprise are: Braveheart Investment; Hotspur Capital Partners; Octopus Investments and Venrex Investment Management.

Leapfrog capital

On this ladder of finance, the danger is that seed investors can fall off and make less money than they should. The risks are relatively high and the funds are relatively small, so they can easily find themselves diluted and replaced.

Ideally, you want spin-outs to have enough resources at their disposal to scale up. At Manchester, the solution has been to create a £32m fund, 10% of which goes on proof of concept and the rest then follows in subsequent rounds. Both the spin-out and the investor gain scale and continuity.

This Premier Fund, which was launched in 2008, is the largest facility of this kind for a single university in Europe. In the Midlands, investors can access a similar source of funding through the Mercia Fund. It offers "pathfinder" grants of up to £250,000, which turn into equity or a royalty when the venture is launched. Mercia then makes a further equity investment in the normal way.

One source of capital that did allow ventures to leapfrog most funding rounds altogether is shut for now. In the early 2000s, several spin-outs raised millions on the London Stock Exchange's market for high-growth, high-risk ventures, AIM, to take their technology all the way through to full commercialisation. In the downturn, there is little sign of such deals making a return as yet.

Corporate venturing, charitable grants

Private investors are not the only players at the early stage of spinning out ideas. Corporates, such as GSK and its SR1 fund, will look at investing at the early stage. Many more, who are committed to speeding up their search for ideas through open innovation, are looking to give spin-outs some scale through revenue-sharing deals.

Another active participant in the market is charities. In healthcare, for instance, the Wellcome Trust acts as a major partner in bringing fundamental research closer to the market. Funds are rarely released directly as cash into your account. They are normally in the form of grants for programmes with conditions attached, often turning a convertible loan when an idea is commercialised.

Spin-outs which rely on charities are often structured as "community interest companies", which are limited by guarantee, but do not pay a dividend. Any profits go back into the business. It is a structure adopted by a team of social scientists at Coventry, for instance, who have created a company to help put young people back to work.

Follow-on capital

Like children leaving home, spin-outs are eventually expected to stand on their own two feet, sending an occasional postcard home and raising funds on normal commercial terms. In business, as in life, it is rare for everything to work out as smoothly as you would like.

Like most parents, Oxford retains an active interest in its offspring. In its finance office, it has a team of two people to manage the equity in their spin-outs. As a supportive shareholder, the University can look at making follow-on investments as required.

The funding package

Even at one of the world's best universities, the process of raising capital for university ventures remains the art of the possible. Says Tom Hockaday:

"We always have an open mind about how to put together a package. We are unlikely to have the luxury of having 10 offers from which to choose. It is a question of putting together a strong offering, then talking to the broadest possible long list."

Clive Rowland at Manchester puts it another way:

> "The trick for us is to identify the right sort of projects and weave in the investment, marketing and entrepreneurial expertise, then start to take a back seat so that the businesses can grow with the right sort of teams in place. Our job then is to go back into the University and assist the transfer of the next set of projects."

For more details on Capital for Enterprise, see www.capitalforenterprise.gov.uk.

PART 6
University profiles and case studies

Profile

Anglia Ruskin
University

Cambridge & Chelmsford

Anglia Ruskin University

Supporting business in today's changing market

Anglia Ruskin University is passionate about the advancement of knowledge and the education of students, and we pride ourselves on taking university education in imaginative new directions. Our key contribution is to the enhancement of social, cultural and economic wellbeing. We provide a range of services aimed at helping organisations connect with our wealth of expert knowledge and expertise.

Consultancy services

We can help guide strategic development, facilitate workforce development through training and continuing professional development, carry out development or testing work in our high-tech laboratories, and offer rapid prototyping, product development, model generation and computer simulations.

Contract, commissioned or collaborative research

We apply professional research techniques to real world problems. Research is carried out to your specific brief and may involve proof of concept, proof of market or market analysis, market research, laboratory testing, data analysis or field studies. Collaborative research is often funded by research councils, government or charities.

Knowledge Transfer Partnerships (KTPs)

A three-way partnership between your business, a leading academic and a talented graduate – working together on your business case. Knowledge Transfer Partnerships enable access to funding, talent and expert subject knowledge. The result can help develop your business for today's market, increase your competitive advantage and improve your business operations and productivity. You benefit from a government grant of up to 67% of the total project cost.

Low carbon KEEP programme

This is a unique programme that supports collaboration between businesses and universities and enables you to improve your competitiveness by working with academic experts and a graduate. Funding is available to small to medium-sized companies within the east of England looking to achieve a significant reduction in their carbon footprint. This could be achieved by developing new products or improving existing products and services, or adapting current processes and changing the way the business operates.

Graduate internship programme

We place recent graduates in businesses in the east of England to work on short-term, strategic projects. It can offer you a flexible and cost-effective resource with long-lasting benefits.

Staff training and development

We deliver work-based and professional development courses to help you support and grow the talent in your organisation. Our clients include organisations such as Harrods, Barclays, Specsavers and UPS. In today's demanding market, building long-term relationships and partnerships with your local university can really help your business grow and compete.

0845 196 3177
business@anglia.ac.uk
http://business.anglia.ac.uk

Case study

Knowledge Transfer Partnership project at Cornelius graded as "outstanding"

The KTP project between Hertfordshire-based chemical distribution and manufacturing company Cornelius Group Plc and Anglia Ruskin University, has been awarded the highest grade of "outstanding" by the KTP National Grading Panel for its outcomes.

The project aimed to implement a business development and marketing capability across the business, and develop both existing and new international marketing strategies. As a result of the project, a clear marketing strategy was devised, allowing the company to grow and diversify against the background of the recent recession.

Darren Spiby, sales director at Cornelius says: "Just a few of the great value creating differences made include: an industry first 'virtual' cosmetics exhibition; a market entry plan for our Polish business, which has identified further expansion opportunities; focussed communications to our customers, which not only keep them informed but also inspire them to buy our products; and 'voice of the customer' surveys, which have been invaluable in helping us improve our service."

The project, managed by Anglia Ruskin University marketing graduate Natalia McDonough, has delivered significant strategic outcomes to the company. Long-term business structures were implemented by identifying new revenue streams and by researching opportunities to expand the existing offer into new areas. The previously sales-led organisation adopted a fresh marketing strategy which created a new "dynamic organisation" and led to a sustainable source of competitive advantage for the company.

The project was also crucial for the success of a new business entity, Cornelius operations in Poland. The partnership enabled Cornelius to leverage their operational capabilities across business groups, perfect the sales support service and achieve significant cost savings through consolidating their supply chain. Such impressive outcomes were achieved within the relatively short period of 21 months, during the difficult economic climate of global recession, making the partnership's achievements even more significant. Cornelius' chairman, Dr Neville Prior, reflected: "This enhanced capability has allowed even stronger relationships to blossom with principals, and through the aim of working with our customers to grow their business with sustainable, quality-assured products, Cornelius has seen excellent progress. Our market entry plans outside of the UK ensure that Cornelius remains a vibrant and exciting company to work for and to work with."

Knowledge Transfer Partnerships are one of the Technology Strategy Board's flagship UK-wide programmes, enabling businesses from all sectors to improve their competitiveness, productivity and performance. KTPs achieve this by helping businesses to access knowledge, technology or skills from UK universities. Jan Stringer, KTP regional adviser, commented: "I witnessed the exceptional teamwork among the Anglia Ruskin team, Natalia (the graduate) and the Cornelius directors. The outstanding results achieved are a testament to the vision and support of the company, the graduate's hard work and Anglia Ruskin University's expert guidance."

Profile

Birmingham City University

With innovative training, talented graduates and a strong track record in sharing our expertise with business, Birmingham City University is well-placed to help any small or medium-sized enterprise to succeed. With over 2,500 staff, the University is one of the largest employers in Birmingham, directly supporting more than 3,000 jobs in the city and contributing approximately £100m to its economy each year.

We make a significant contribution to business growth by providing consultancy and partnership services, sharing academic expertise and graduate talent. Our Knowledge Transfer Partnerships involve a graduate working inside a company or organisation, drawing on their own knowledge and experience, and that of the wider University.

Our partners range from household names such as Microsoft and the BBC to smaller businesses such as gardening and giftware supplier Marvell's and "virtual world" specialists Daden. Our excellence in the arts means we have exceptional links with the creative industries while, in the automotive field, students have been involved in projects ranging from designing component systems for off-road karts to environmental initiatives with Morgan Motor Company.

The Interiors and Lifestyle Futures project saw us provide help to companies looking to expand into these high-value markets, whilst our Jewellery Industry Innovation Centre supports the sector through research, training, mentoring and consultancy. Our Faculty of Health has pioneered e-learning in areas such as moving and handling, benefiting SMEs as well as larger health organisations.

We provide innovative training solutions, tailored to the needs of particular industries and clients. We launched the UK's first-ever foundation degree in builders merchanting, deliver specialised training for managers in the pub and restaurant industry and have been recognised by the government for our pioneering professional development for the computer games industry.

Central to our expertise is our team of academics, who helped us achieve one of the biggest improvements of any university in the latest Research Assessment Exercise audit. We have made our biggest commitment yet to develop our research profile by launching a five-year research strategy and investing in 12 Centres of Excellence.

We produce skilled and employable students and graduates, offering industry-inspired recruitment and selection services to ensure businesses get the right candidate. This has resulted in 83% of graduates entering employment or further study within six months of graduation (*Destinations survey 2009/10*) and we are in the top 20 UK universities for the most students in graduate-level jobs (*Sunday Times University Guide 2011*).

Over the past 10 years, we have worked with over 5,000 SMEs and our continued success is testimony to our support of, and commitment to, smaller businesses.

0121 331 5252
business.services@bcu.ac.uk
www.bcu.ac.uk/business

Case study

Melissa Leong, a student on Birmingham City Business School's MBA Finance course was placed with CW Corporate Communications Ltd – an SME business which provided internal and external communications solutions for a wide range of clients – to develop and embed a strategic financial management system for the company, as well as overseeing improvements in its business processes in order to help increase efficiency and improve competitiveness.

Melissa drove forward the company's efforts to achieve ISO9001 quality accreditation, which officially recognised its commitment to customer service and continuous improvement. As well as helping businesses to improve their own efficiency and profitability, the accreditation can also give them advantages through preferred status for tenders and lower insurance premiums.

In addition, she took a lead role in the company's introduction of a customer relationship management (CRM) system and helped to develop and support its future strategy using strategic management tools.

The changes managed by Melissa helped the business to keep a tighter control on costs, enabling it to record an increase in profits even when turnover fell during the recession.

CW Corporate Communications managing director Nigel Curtis said: "Melissa has been instrumental in establishing, and taking control of, financial reporting at CW with monthly management accounts and profitability reviews. This information proved invaluable for the directors in controlling costs during the recession to the extent that we actually improved our gross profit margin when turnover fell by 25%.

"Further successes have been a complete overhaul of all our internal processes and procedures towards achieving ISO9001 accreditation, the introduction of a CRM system to aid new business development and strategic support at board level across all decision-making.

"Melissa is self-starting and focused on the task in hand at all times and is professional, conscientious, reliable and enthusiastic in her work and in her dealings with colleagues. She is easily one of the top three young managers I have been privileged to work with in more than 25 years in business.

"Melissa took a pragmatic approach to the potentially complex challenges this role presented. It was clear from her qualifications and experience that she had the knowledge and skills to do the job, and she was also able to explain in practical and simple terms how she would apply these to meet the objectives and requirements of the position. We also felt Melissa's personal style of gentle tenacity would be most effective in driving through the changes that we knew we would have to make in order to benefit from the new systems and processes being introduced."

Profile

cambridge **enterprise**
commercialising University science

University of Cambridge

University of Cambridge people and ideas are at the heart of the Cambridge Phenomenon, one of the world's most productive technology clusters. The economic, social and environmental impact of these companies and the people they attract are evident everywhere.

Cambridge Enterprise, a wholly owned subsidiary of the University, is responsible for commercialising Cambridge research. The company works in partnership with industry to ensure that Cambridge innovation has maximum societal and financial impact. We act as business agents for academics who wish to act as consultants, oversee the licensing of inventions and find vital funding opportunities for early-stage companies.

In the most recent national survey conducted in 2008, Cambridge Enterprise was ranked as the UK's top technology transfer office, and has been highly successful in bringing Cambridge research to the wider world, through consultancy, licensing and spin-out companies.

The sharing of university research leads to incredible advances in technology, bioscience and engineering, bringing huge benefits to society and making a direct impact on the economy by creating new jobs, attracting inward investment and generating sales.

Consultancy Services is an important and effective consultancy service which enables the University to share its knowledge with government, industry and the public sector and make a direct impact on society. Our goal is to make the process of consultancy easier for academics and the organisations in need of their expertise. Our service covers the administrative issues associated with consultancy projects, including negotiation of contract terms and conditions, arrangements for use of university facilities, invoicing, debt collection and income distribution. Examples of the types of consultancy projects undertaken include: technical and creative solutions to specific business problems, provision of expert reports on technical, economic and commercial issues, expert witness advice and serving on scientific advisory boards.

Technology Transfer involves management and licensing of intellectual property, and provides access to proof of concept funding for the development of early stage inventions. Licensing Cambridge research to existing companies is the core of Cambridge Enterprise's business, and licensing has led to innumerable financial and societal benefits. Successes include Campath®, an effective treatment for chronic lymphocytic leukaemia which shows great potential as a treatment for multiple sclerosis; and CASTEP, a computer-based materials simulation toolkit which is used worldwide in a wide range of industries.

Cambridge Enterprise seed funds provide access to early stage capital through the three evergreen seed funds it manages on the University's behalf. This early stage capital and support is pivotal to success of new technology companies in what is often seen as a high-risk section of the investment spectrum. Since seed funding began in 1995, our portfolio companies have raised over £600m in further investment and grant funding. They now employ close to 2,000 people and generate an annual turnover of £170m.

01223 760339
enquiries@enterprise.cam.ac.uk
www.enterprise.cam.ac.uk

Case study

Retirement and risk

As more and more pension schemes are closed or scaled back, individuals are being asked to take an increasingly active role in their financial planning for retirement. The public at large has a relatively low level of financial literacy, and there is a constantly widening gulf between this and the knowledge required to accurately assess the complicated credit, insurance and investment products which are available in ever-increasing numbers.

The problem faced by providers of online financial planning tools is not poorly made decisions on the part of their customers, but decisions that are not made at all. Most employees are not helped by their access to pension sites: they either fail to use the sites at all, or make poor decisions when they do use them. Various biases, so-called "maths trauma", a widespread lack of financial literacy and labyrinthine financial websites can all lead to either poor financial decisions or decision avoidance on the part of the consumer.

The American financial services firm Black Rock requested an assessment of Target Plan, its online financial planning tool, from international consulting firm Towers Perrin (now Towers Watson) who in turn sought the advice of a group of leading Cambridge academics.

Consultancy Services contracted with Towers Perrin for the services of Dr John Coates of Judge Business School, Dr Michael Aitken of the Department of Experimental Psychology, and Professor David Spiegelhalter of the Department of Pure Mathematics and Mathematical Statistics, to consider and report on the various reasons which discourage the public from using online financial planning tools, and suggest improvements to Black Rock's Target Plan website.

Following the completion of the initial project, Towers Watson contracted with Consultancy Services for the services of Dr Coates and his colleagues to assist in the design and review process of an employee portal for Black Rock itself, to encourage its own employees to view important information more frequently.

It is hoped that the project will help to design better communications and tools to engage employees and their customers, and enable them to make better-informed investment decisions.

Profile

City University London

CITY UNIVERSITY LONDON

City University London is one of the capital's leading universities, situated close to the City of London. We are focused on business and the professions and help companies of all sizes access new knowledge, cutting-edge expertise and fresh ideas.

We recognise the needs and ambitions of both start-up and established companies. Our researchers are actively engaged in developing new technologies and understanding how businesses can succeed in a rapidly changing market.

City has a wealth of business knowledge and hands-on commercial experience in a variety of research areas, including: aeronautical engineering and aviation safety systems; automotive and energy systems; cloud computing and website usability; colour vision testing and screening in workplace and schools; expert witness training; GIS and special mapping; journalism and media; medical devices; risk modeling; sensor technology; software coding, testing and de-bugging.

Our services for business include the follwing.

- **Research services:** our academics can undertake a specific piece of research on your behalf or help resolve scientific or technical challenges of strategic importance to your organisation.

- **Expert advice and consultancy:** we can offer valuable advice to help solve your technical or managerial problems.

- **Business incubation:** the London City Incubator helps early-stage high-growth start-up businesses to prepare for investment by engaging the commercial skills of Cass MBA students.

- **Commercial opportunities:** form a joint venture with us or invest in one of our exciting spin-outs.

- **Staff development:** we offer a variety of professional development programmes from short courses to Continuing Professional Development and Enterprise Education.

- **Student placements and graduate recruitment:** our graduates have up-to-date knowledge and practical experience. Alternatively, Knowledge Transfer Partnership, a leading graduate recruitment programme, can help boost your competitive advantage.

We recognise that each company has its own particular requirements and we tailor our services accordingly.

We are always delighted to talk with local businesses and entrepreneurs. Please feel free to contact us:

Research & Enterprise
City University London
Northampton Square
London
EC1V 0HB

0207 040 8096
business@city.ac.uk
www.city.ac.uk/for-business

Case study

From academia to industry

Among the many projects Professor Ahmed Kovacevic from City's School of Engineering and Mathematical Sciences is currently establishing with wider industrial partners are the research and development (R&D) activities of Howden Compressors Ltd, a major UK compressor manufacturer.

As the Chair of Engineering Design and Compressor Technology in the School of Engineering and Mathematical Sciences, Professor Kovacevic has set up a comprehensive R&D programme at Howden that aims to establish the company's technological advantage and to increase current business opportunities by developing new products.

As a result of this prolific collaboration the company has doubled in size in just two years by combining its inherent know-how and manufacturing excellence with City's licensed intellectual property.

Jim Fairbairn OBE, Managing Director of Howden Compressors Ltd says: "Howden Compressors has extensively used innovation to differentiate and expand its business reach. Collaboration with city University London and particularly with Professor Kovacevic has contributed significantly to the management's ambitious strategy for growth in supplying products and services to major mature and developing markets throughout the world."

City's short course helps a start-up to find success

Several successful enterprises have emerged as a direct result of individuals attending City's short courses. Among them is Bea's of Bloomsbury – an independent café and pastry shop that has quickly become one of the worst-kept secrets in foodie London.

Owner-manager Bea Vo trained as a pastry chef in acclaimed restaurants such as Nobu and Asia de Cuba before setting up her business in 2008 with just two full-time employees... including herself.

Since completing the Starting up in Business course at City, Bea has expanded her business to employ some 22 staff and has recently opened a second outlet within the prestigious One New Change shopping centre opposite St Paul's Cathedral in London.

Find our more about our short courses at www.city.ac.uk/shortcourses.

Profile

Coventry University

Coventry University has always believed in working closely with industrial partners, be they local businesses, national companies or multi-national corporations, and we are proud to be seen as a "business-facing" university.

Coventry is the number one university in the UK for working with business; in 2010–11 alone over 9,000 SMEs benefited from numerous regeneration and development programmes delivered by the University, consequently creating jobs and businesses across the UK.

Coventry University also works alongside industry partners to tackle complex real-world challenges. The recently launched "grand challenge initiatives" concentrate on research that has real tangible and practical gains which make an impact on society, and improves the way we live. Six key global issues have been identified where the University's research expertise can have a significant impact.

The six core grand challenges are as follows.

1. Integrated transport and logistics: improving transport services and the movement of people and goods.

2. Digital media: supporting the commercial exploitation of digital systems.

3. Ageing society: supporting broad societal issues affecting a growing population of older people.

4. Sustainable agriculture and food: developing sustainable agriculture and food systems.

5. Low carbon vehicles: designing, testing and evaluating low carbon vehicles and systems.

6. Low impact buildings: increasing innovation in the sustainable construction industry.

These initiatives enable Coventry University to work in partnership with industry to address the large social and economical challenges of the 21st century. Coventry University has an excellent reputation for effective implementation of a full range of knowledge-based sustainable business solutions – enabling enterprises to compete in today's global economy. These include supporting start-up companies, accessing research funds, partnership creation (within the UK and overseas), capability development, acquisition of business innovation skills, business mentoring, and the commercial exploitation of intellectual assets, products and services in the UK and overseas.

Contact: Sophie Bauer
07974 984733
sbauer@cad.coventry.ac.uk

Case study

Developing innovative new products with business

The walking aid market in the UK has been very slow to develop and embrace good product design. However, far-reaching changes made to healthcare commissioning and the adoption of the "personalisation agenda", have now opened opportunities for innovative new product improvement. Abianco Ltd, an SME which specialises in the design and development of products for disabled people, was looking to take full advantage of those changes when they approached Coventry University to assist them in developing a number of new features to extend their existing range of walking devices.

Coventry University's Health Design Technology Institute worked in close collaboration with the company over an 18-month period to bring their product ideas to reality, providing support in:

- concept design
- ergonomics
- computer-aided design (CAD) modelling
- 3D rendering
- prototyping
- end-user evaluation and testing
- product promotion and showcasing
- introductions to manufacturers and distributors.

As a result of this collaboration, Abianco Ltd's new product range was launched at Naidex, the UK's largest homecare, disability and rehabilitation event, in April 2011. Discussions are now taking place with major distributors in the UK and European mainland, as well as further afield to get the product into the global marketplace.

Helping business to gain competitive advantage

Coventry-based SME Reports4Property Ltd is a certified surveying service for commercial and residential properties. Following the UK recession they saw a downturn in property survey sales. They recognised the need to evolve their product offering to distinguish themselves from their competitors through a rebranding exercise.

Coventry University provided funding through their economic challenge investment fund, enabling Reports4Property to purchase expert design and marketing support from specialists from the Design Institute, at Coventry University.

The Design Institute produced a visibility strategy and professional marketing material to promote the new brand – Midland Surveyors. Core messages were created to ensure a smooth transition in company identity, and a logo and associated images were designed alongside a new website and promotional literature.

Armed with a revitalised brand and evolved product offering, Midland Surveyors now faces the future in a stronger competitive position. Their new offerings include powerful sales tools for their clients to use, such as virtual tours and online floor-plans.

Says Len Cannon, Director of Reports4Property Ltd: "Coventry University were quick to assimilate our present situation along with the threats and challenges facing our business. They provided valuable input into and ultimately created the marketing infrastructure to carry our business forward. The whole process was made all more enjoyable by the team's proactive approach, humour and professionalism."

Profile

University of Cumbria

The University of Cumbria is a new university, but with a long history. We opened our doors in 2007 after a number of successful higher education institutions came together to form the newest university in England. It means we are new, but have a long heritage of teaching students, and working with businesses and our local, regional, national and international communities. A strategic goal of the University is to support business and entrepreneurship, helping boost the regional economy and raise the level of competitiveness of businesses.

In terms of our history, St Martin's College was the largest of the institutions which went on to form our university. Founded in 1964 to train teachers, it grew over the years and developed a fine reputation for the quality of its teacher and health professional training, opening a campus in Carlisle along the way, as well as taking over Charlotte Mason College in Ambleside in the Lake District which was founded in 1896, and influenced generations of educators.

The former Cumbria Institute of the Arts can trace its history back to 1822 when the Society for the Encouragement of Fine Arts was formed in Carlisle. It became the only specialist institute of the arts in north-west England and one of only a small number of such institutions in the country. Recent alumni include Turner Prize winner Keith Turner, actor Charlie Hunnam, Gerard McKeown, performance poet and ceramicist, Tom Hopkins Gibson, recently commissioned by Liberty of London. Graphic design, digital art, film and TV production and journalism are now core areas of expertise, to the benefit of students, but also in terms of offering knowledge and expertise to local businesses to support their growth.

The legacy of the University also holds a long history in agricultural training. Today we are home to the National School of Forestry, the Centre for Wildlife Conservation and our outdoor studies courses – more outdoor students study with us than any other higher education institution in Europe. Our Centre of Excellence in Leadership Development provides a host of cutting-edge leadership and management programmes, including our MBA, but also programmes developed for small and medium-sized employers and bespoke solutions, which enable businesses to improve their performance.

In West Cumbria we are a key player in the development of Britain's Energy Coast™ by providing courses for individuals and businesses at our state-of-the-art Learning Gateway West. Our newest degree in sustainable engineering is soon to be launched, responding to the needs of local businesses. Gateway buildings in Ambleside, Carlisle, Lancaster, Barrow and London complete the portfolio of contemporary learning and teaching environments – used by students and businesses alike.

Contact:
Dr Michele Lawty-Jones
07740 248800

Case study

Brathay Trust

Brathay Trust is a leading national outdoor training charity established over 65 years ago. Specialists in experiential learning and based at the edge of Lake Windermere, Brathay works with the most vulnerable and disadvantaged young people to help them develop the skills, confidence and motivation to make positive choices in their lives. They also work with a diverse range of businesses and organisations, offering bespoke residential programmes in areas such as team building, management and leadership.

The Knowledge Transfer Partnership, a two-year partnership between Brathay Trust and the University of Cumbria, funded by the Technology Strategy Board, commenced in July 2010 to support the development of a research function to formalise commitment to research and evaluation.

The KTP at Brathay provides an employed "associate" to link between experts at the University and the needs of the charity to carry out the project. Karen Stuart, the associate for the Brathay project, is working as the Research Practice Lead on the project. Karen is using the knowledge and expertise of university academics to support the objectives the project. These include the following.

- Providing an organisation wide strategic approach to research and evaluation activity.

- Developing areas of research activities such as assessing the impact of their work over longer timescales.

- Developing programmes offered at Brathay and promoting them nationally.

- Increasing Brathay's profile and market share through the use of impact data.

The KTP was the catalyst for the securing of a further £500,000 of funding through the Cabinet Office, which will support the next stage of the KTP, including the employment of a research assistant and several research internships to develop the research and evaluation strategy, market research, six pilot projects, a national conference and enhanced IT infrastructure.

Chris Loynes at the University said: "We are delighted for Brathay and pleased to be associated with such a worthwhile charity. Our expertise lies in the research of the latest thinking and teaching practices as well as specialist knowledge in the analysis of research data in relation to the transition of young people in British society such as trends in youth culture, offending, education, employment and social mobility. This makes us ideally placed to work with Brathay on this particular project."

Godfrey Owen, CEO of Brathay, said: "The funding we have managed to secure is an excellent achievement for us and will help us to realise our full research potential. The government is currently going through a funding review and this money will support the charity through the transition."

Associate Karen Stuart, pictured above, has developed 10 literature reviews and plans are in place to publish these. In addition to this, she has been a guest speaker at a number of national conferences.

Profile

University for the Creative Arts

UCA

university for the **creative arts**

The University for the Creative Arts (UCA) has campuses in
Canterbury, Epsom, Farnham, Maidstone and Rochester and is one of Europe's largest specialist
universities of art, design, architecture, media and communication.

Supporting business for innovation and growth

The enterprise team acts as a first point of call for our work with business and the local community,
promoting our extensive resources to develop your new products and services. As a specialist art
and design institution UCA provides a dynamic, creative environment with individuals who possess
extensive experience and expertise across the entire creative sector.

Access to creative consultants

Creativity is essential in business and helps to create a real distinctiveness in the market. The Edge
Consultancy at the University for the Creative Arts provides knowledge, expert advice and creative
insights to support your business development.

Edge offers consultancy, sector speakers and bespoke training on a broad range of subject areas
from business skills to use of specialist software. To access our extensive list of experts' profiles visit:
www.ucaedge.com.

Access to specialist equipment

Need access to specialist and expensive equipment? We offer access to a range of technology,
including rapid prototyping and digital textile printing and the latest in 3D scanning and filming.
Supported by skilled technicians and consultants, we can help make your idea a commercial reality.

Bespoke in-house training

We have a range of courses which can be adapted and delivered on businesses premises, providing
bespoke training, from business skills to training in the use of specialist software.

Knowledge Transfer Partnerships – partnership between a business, graduate and an academic to
solve a business problem.

Live projects/Work Placement/Internships – tangible benefits to business and students.

The creative challenge

The creative challenge is an established annual competition that demands the best from our
students. You can get involved by:

- being a mentor
- providing a student work placement
- sponsorship: we have various packages where you can benefit from a dynamic and
  profitable relationship with one of the UK's top arts
  universities.

For more information visit www.creativechallenge.info.

enterpriseoffice@ucreative.ac.uk
www.ucreative.ac.uk/enterprise

Case study

Funzee gets wise to size

Funzee Limited is a growing clothing design and manufacture enterprise that specialises in a unique product in the UK market – the Funzee, a soft, cosy, all-in-one suit for adults to wear as a sleep or lounge garment. The company's distinctive product and informal, engaging and fun marketing tone have gained an increasing number of buyers. It has secured different types of client across the UK, including the student and music festival market.

The problem

Mark, the company owner says: "I have experience of marketing on the internet so a simple website was an easy way of testing whether there was interest and demand for a product. It became apparent that there was a demand so I needed to think more seriously about sizing, fabrics, designs etc, all things about which I know nothing. I approached Edge and they appointed Denise Ward to assist me."

The solution

Denise says: "Initially I addressed inconsistencies in how the product had been sized, introducing a different size base, based on height, which helped clarify and standardise Funzee's sizing policy." Another important issue was the visibility of Funzee's sizing policy to potential customers. This was easily addressed by creating a readable table of the newly standardised sizing elements and uploading it on to Funzee's website.

The benefits

Mark says: "Initially Denise helped me to make my sizing more 'scientific'. As a result of Denise's advice, our return rate has been much reduced, as people are now buying the size that is correct for them." With a solid foundation in terms of sizing, Mark has gained the confidence to research other ranges of clothing and launch new products. Denise continues to advise Mark across a variety of issues: sizing, fabric choice, production specifications and processes.

The Edge consultant Denise Ward is a production management tutor in fashion. She has broad industry experience, including 13 years as a production manager at Karen Millen.

Denise's profile and that of our other experts is available at www.ucaedge.com.

Profile

University of Derby

The University of Derby offers a flexible approach to work-based learning. Primarily, the University recognises that their delegates are very busy individuals. SMEs have many pressures which are not only financial but generally time-based. To ensure that delegates get the best value from their learning experience, University of Derby Corporate (UDC) offers various opportunities to enable the delegate to achieve their required learning outcomes.

One particular way of engaging with learners is by using bite-sized sessions that build up a portfolio over time. This enables the learner to manage their own time and include it into their busy schedule of operating at a new or growing enterprise. Bite-sized modules can be supplemented with additional online learning modules that are specific to their own learning needs; whilst the partnership developed with the learner continues to grow and adapt to their own personal development plan.

UDC also offer full programmes which can be either accredited or not. These programmes can be delivered to a group of businesses who have a common development need. This approach offers more choice to SMEs and yet remains economically viable for UDC to deliver. These programmes may consist of classroom and online learning platforms. The experience that the University of Derby has developed over the years in delivering training and education solutions to a variety of organisations has enabled it to understand client needs.

The use of work-based projects are paramount to the success of learning whilst at work. Many of the challenges SMEs and their employees face provide ideal real-life case studies that can enable the delegate to meet the learning outcomes of the program by understanding and reflecting on the experience. UDC supports delegates throughout their programme to ensure they stay on track and meet their initial objectives. This is an essential component of the process because it enables the delegate to maintain motivation and confidence in their ability to learn.

Another important area where UDC helps SMEs is by providing solutions through consultancy-based projects and/or provision of specific expertise that is either unobtainable or economically unviable for the organisation to procure normally. This can be achieved through collaborative programmes such as Knowledge Transfer Partnerships (KTPs) where knowledge is exchanged between both parties enabling a positive outcome for both the University and the company. UDC can also provide access to student placement schemes, again, programmes of mutual benefit which enable organisations to develop new capability and fresh knowledge by tapping into the graduate and undergraduate talent pool.

There are many benefits for SMEs from working directly with the UDC team, the major being the skills and knowledge gained whilst undertaking their normal business and this adds value to the organisation.

0800 678 3311
udc@derby.ac.uk
www.derby.ac.uk/corporate

Case study

Showsec

The events management industry is still maturing and many organisations still depend on largely casual and untrained staff. However, the impact of legislation and the growing professionalism of industry leaders such as Showsec has led to a demand for cost effective staff development. To achieve this Showsec and the University of Derby Corporate (UDC) instigated an effective and mutually beneficial partnership.

The challenge

Showsec were specifically seeking to develop the leadership and communication skills of their supervisory and management cohort. This presented a number of challenges, including the diverse educational background of those taking part, and the operational demands, requiring a flexible and efficiently delivered programme.

Solution

The programme design of the Foundation Degree developed accurately reflects the client's requirements. It covers personal development, event safety management, leadership, communication and how to develop staff. The programme is built around the principles of work based learning with all of the case studies, workshops and assessments being built around real workplace scenarios. This ensures that the learning is not just relevant but is directly applicable in the workplace.

The outcome

The developing relationship between UDC and Showsec has already delivered benefits to both partners. Showsec has been accredited by the University as a delivery partner so that Showsec staff can now deliver elements of the development programme. In addition the leadership credibility of both partners within the events management industry has improved with the partnership being showcased at recent work based learning conferences.

Profile

University of East London

The University of East London (UEL) is a global learning community with 23,000 students from over 120 countries world-wide. Our vision is to achieve recognition, both nationally and internationally, as a successful and inclusive regional university proud of its diversity. We are committed to new modes of learning which focus on students and enhance their employability, and are renowned for our contribution to social, cultural and economic development, especially through our research and scholarship. We have a strong track-record in widening participation and working with industry.

Rated among the top three modern universities for research in London and top 10 modern universities in the UK, the University of East London has a reputation for internationally-rated research. Our substantial base of research expertise enables us to provide the latest business thinking, technology and skills in a wide range of disciplines to industry and enables us to provide organisations with new insights into their operations and/or solutions to the challenges they face.

Our research expertise broadly falls into six key themes:

1. creative, digital and information technology
2. children, education and lifelong learning
3. sport, health and wellbeing
4. sustainability
5. social equality and justice, human rights and security
6. politics, culture and society.

The university has engaged in a multitude of consultancy and contract research projects, ranging from consultancy projects with local SMEs and multinationals through to contract research projects with government departments.

We help businesses develop their ideas and capabilities through a number of approaches, such as engaging with them on European Regional Development Fund (ERDF) innovation projects, though to flagship knowledge exchange projects such as KTPs.

The university also offers a wide portfolio of student placement projects that connects companies to talented students and graduates to deliver short-term business projects, such as developing new websites, conducting market research and new product development.

The Knowledge Dock Business Centre (KDBC), located in the newly appointed Royal Docks Enterprise Zone, is the only EU accredited business innovation centre (BIC) in London. The centre houses 43 modern business offices, shared office space, light industrial units as well as HotHatch, a dedicated hot-desking facility. What truly differentiates the KDBC from other serviced offices in the area is the on-site advice, training, wealth of knowledge and expertise that being situated within a university can bring to a business.

020 8223 7776
reds@uel.ac.uk
www.uel.ac.uk

Case study

Alexandra Kelly started Powerchex in 2004, after realising the need for pre-employment screening in the financial services sector. A few months after the company was founded Alexandra became aware of the University of East London (UEL) and the services they provide. Since then Powerchex have taken part in a variety of collaborative knowledge exchange projects with the University as the company has rapidly expanded.

In their first summer, when Powerchex had just two employees, the company took part in the "shell step" programme, as Alexandra knew that taking part in a highly regarded programme would give the company an aura of respectability. Since then the company has engaged with UEL on a number of student placement projects to help raise the profile of Powerchex. As a direct result of the projects, the company has been featured in most of the national broadsheets, including the *Financial Times*, the *Guardian* and Alexandra was also interviewed on BBC News.

On the back of the success of these projects, Powerchex has collaborated with UEL on a number of funded projects, including a London Development Agency (LDA) funded programme, "secondment into knowledge", which helped to streamline the company's processes, as well as a number of European Regional Development Funded (ERDF) innovation projects that were aimed at developing the company's service offer and raising the company's profile.

More recently Powerchex, which has won a multitude of awards, has partnered with the University on a Knowledge Transfer Partnership project to develop an innovative online tool. Currently in the final stages of the project, Alexandra says:

"It has been a huge success and has directly resulted in winning a large client and a large American company has also bought the business. We wanted to create an up-to-date, well put together online form – a customised tool for all clients. It can reduce the workload of financial companies by 50%."

On her experience of working with UEL, Alexandra said: "There are no negatives. As a small business you have the ability to use the University and the tremendous wealth of knowledge, expertise and resources it has to offer. We have got so much out of it without the big consultancy fees you would expect if you engaged with a private consultancy company, it is like having an R&D department that you call upon when your company needs it. The standard of help is really good; business owners should get involved with universities. They need to find out what is available; it will give them a good competitive edge. Everyone at the University of East London is commercially driven – it is a key aspect of making it all work."

Profile

University of Greenwich

The University of Greenwich has a wealth of resources, skilled people and business support services that can be utilised to help your business. The Greenwich Research & Enterprise (GRE) office can help you to access these and work with you on your business development.

No matter the size of your company we can direct you on how to improve your business practices, find suitable training schemes, gain access to funded research opportunities, find suitable student and graduate workers and provide business development advice and problem solving.

To help you find the service or solution your company needs we have a team of specialised business development managers (BDMs). They will be your primary contact and guide you through your project or request. Our BDMs work within the schools and can help you to more swiftly find a solution tailored to your needs.

The University of Greenwich has worked with clients ranging from small businesses to large multi-nationals. As well as working with household names such as Boeing, Cadbury's, GlaxoSmithKline, the NHS and the World Bank, we also work with start-ups and SMEs such as Fudge Kitchen and Carbon8. Says Sian Holt, Manager, Fudge Kitchen, "The great part of having the University of Greenwich work with us was putting their scientific expertise into practice to our benefit."

GRE services

We aim to tailor our service to businesses so that you can more easily find what you require from our wide range of support and services for business.

Our business services include business development, problem solving, consultancy, technology development, special facilities and equipment and access to funding.

Our employer services include government-subsidised funding, Knowledge Transfer Partnerships, training and development, staffing and support and student placements.

We support local business, entrepreneurs and local people committed to turning their ideas and inventions into businesses by offering serviced offices, mentoring and access to resources.

Business and research

The University of Greenwich places particular value on applied research and collaborations with industry and commerce, as well as the public sector.

Supporting our objective to be a research-informed university, we have been experiencing some of the fastest growth in research income from industry in the sector, and are one of the leading modern universities in terms of the value of research with businesses. Finding collaborative opportunities to work with small and large businesses allows us to apply our expertise and offer these benefits to the businesses we work with.

Research & Enterprise (GRE) Office
020 8331 7867
enterprise@gre.ac.uk
www.gre.ac.uk/enterprise

Case study

Sian Holt had been successfully running Jim Garrahy's Fudge Kitchen in the UK for 25 years. The company makes all its 20 flavours of fudge by hand in its shops, so customers can see it being made and know that they are buying a fresh product.

The problem

However, plans to supply the product wholesale to farm shops, delicatessens and other retail outlets had been hampered by the relatively short shelf-life of the fudge. Unlike many other types of fudge Sian's does not contain butter, which means that after it has been made it needs to be eaten within a week.

Determined to extend the shelf-life, Sian looked at many options including different packaging; however, none were successful. Then, following an internet search, she came across expertise available at the University of Greenwich.

Finding and funding a solution

Food safety expert Linda Nicolaides is from the University's Natural Resources Institute (NRI), which is based at its Medway campus in Chatham Maritime. Together with Sian, she successfully applied for the Fudge Kitchen to be part of the South East England Development Agency's (SEEDA) Business Plus scheme, a Knowledge Transfer Programme.

Food technologist Julie Crenn, a recent graduate from NRI's MSc in Food Safety & Quality Management, was chosen as the KTP associate to help with the research and received funding to try to help solve the Fudge Kitchen's shelf-life extension dilemma.

Splitting her time between the Canterbury shop and University of Greenwich laboratories, Julie looked at different natural ingredients that might help prolong the life of the fudge but she had a strict brief to follow.

Benefits and impact

Fudge Kitchen did not want the appearance, taste or texture of the fudge to change as they are unique selling points. After extensive research, Julie recommended a change to the sugar levels in the product, which didn't affect its overall quality or taste but did allow it to have a shelf-life of more than three weeks. Julie went on to teach Fudge Kitchen staff across the country how to make the new recipe.

Sian is now wholesaling her products to other retail outlets and restaurants and turnover looks set to add more than £200,000 to Fudge Kitchen's bottom line.

Profile

Heriot-Watt University

Increasingly the role of universities in supporting their national and local economies is being recognised and is translating into practical support for small companies whether it is a redesign of business processes or introduction of new products. In addition, a university will often have an established relationship with a multinational company with which smaller companies work, or wish to work, and the university can enhance or facilitate the B2B interaction.

The traditional role of a university is to create and disseminate knowledge so it follows that universities are in a position of strength to play a crucial role in wealth creation on two fronts; by sharing their knowledge with businesses large and small, and by turning the solution to a research question into a commercial enterprise that will grow and prosper.

Working with industry has always been a core activity for Heriot-Watt University. We offer a real exchange of knowledge and understanding aimed at developing and supporting companies' long-term strategies rather than simply "pushing" technology and raw ideas at companies.

We have expanded our ability to help business find novel solutions to problems by developing a package that facilitates interaction with companies through business development staff, a programme to enhance academic skills in working with companies and a programme to grow robust new companies based on our technology, all supported by a major investment in marketing and events. Combined these elements have proven they can increase interactions and ensure long-term and beneficial outcomes for companies. Access is easy; companies can link to us through a variety of mechanisms — industrial collaborations, joint industry partnerships, technology licensing, Continuing Professional Development and consultancy services.

A team of business development executives (BDEs) is embedded in key areas where we excel, including petroleum engineering, engineering and the physical sciences, energy, built environment, life sciences, transport, finance, computing and design. Our BDEs facilitate your contact with an academic to find the solution you need. They can suggest improvements to processes by offering research ideas and technology at reasonable terms, data analysis and assistance with accessing funding from a variety of sources in the UK and Europe.

Heriot-Watt's commitment to addressing leading-edge business solutions is demonstrated by our desire to grow our user-focused research and leadership in industrial research. Our James Watt Institute for High Value Manufacturing, Scotland's first Innovative Manufacturing Research Centre (IMRC), provides a focus for research excellence in areas underpinning manufacturing and the digital economy. It facilitates active collaboration with local, UK and international companies and its effective knowledge transfer makes an important contribution to the economy.

0131 451 3070
res@hw.ac.uk
www.hw.ac.uk/industry

Case study

Micro-optics: custom spectacles make lasers brighter

PowerPhotonic is an innovative Scottish technology company which designs and manufactures custom micro-optics for beam enhancement of laser diodes arrays in bars and stacks, providing unique optical solutions using rapidly manufactured optical components.

The next generation of optical data storage and solid state laser pumping have contributed to laser diodes becoming a billion dollar industry. The ability to offer increased brightness, wider operating temperature range and higher efficiencies has also enabled penetration into the defence and medical sectors. There is a business need and a constant requirement to increase product performance, while reducing cost and power consumption.

Responding to these needs, the Laser and Photonics Applications (LPA) Group at Heriot-Watt University, led by Professor Howard Baker, has pioneered the production of custom micro-optics by laser micro-machining and polishing; applying detailed understanding of laser machining techniques to produce functional optics with arbitrary surface shapes.

The results of this research have led to the formation of high tech spin-out company, PowerPhotonic Ltd. The company has developed its research into world-leading micro-optical fabrication technology that enables it to compete in high power industrial laser and optical communications markets.

The ability to design and produce innovative micro-optics at a UK fabrication facility has allowed the LPA Group to press ahead with a range of demonstrations of new capabilities for diode laser sources, far beyond the original application in correction of beam errors. In collaboration with industrial partner, Selex Sensors and Airborne Systems, the group has demonstrated the use of the arbitrary surface-shape capability optics fabrication to produce optical elements which directly convert the beams of a linear array of emitters into hexagonal close-packed formats suitable for future mid-infrared laser sources. The fabrication of the optical component for this application was carried out by PowerPhotonic.

In parallel work under a Technology Strategy Board project, with GSI Ltd of Rugby, PowerPhotonic and Cranfield University, PowerPhotonic is building modules using the laser beam shaping technique as part of the development of multi-kilowatt lasers for welding applications.

Joint Innovative Manufacturing Research Centre (IMRC) work with PowerPhotonic and Heriot-Watt University's James Watt Institute has developed a range of products where the original beam correction capability is combined with a second optical function, usually array beam collimation, on one laser-cut substrate reducing the complexity of the beam line in high-brightness diode laser products.

Roy McBride, Managing Director of PowerPhotonic stated: "The James Watt Institute's IMRC has not only allowed us to advance our research, but we have successfully satisfied real business requirements with a commercial solution."

Profile

University of Huddersfield

The University of Huddersfield has a strong track record of working with companies across a variety of business sectors, including engineering, automotive, transport, chemical, biomedical, health, creative industries, digital and media.

These partnerships work in many different ways and we are keen to develop links with more businesses. We understand business needs and drivers and we believe that effective collaboration requires familiarity, trust and confidence. We can work with you to define your interests and identify opportunities for collaboration.

Partnerships can follow many routes ranging from R&D projects, tailored consultancy services as well as a wide range of training and development opportunities which can range across subject areas, levels, duration and flexibility.

All our services to businesses draw upon the specialist knowledge from across our multidisciplinary leading-edge research base, and utilise our academics' knowledge and hands-on experience to find innovative solutions for business problems. This includes such areas as expert opinion and advice, expert witness and testing and analysis.

The University of Huddersfield is one of the UK's top 10 providers of "sandwich" courses where students undertake a paid work placement in industry. Placement students can bring up-to-date skills and ideas, as well as a fresh perspective to businesses at a relatively low cost. We also have a long track record of successful Knowledge Transfer Partnerships (KTPs). Partial funding is available for these three-way partnerships involving a business, a recent graduate and academic staff, where the graduate works on a strategic project.

Our wealth of expertise covers many different disciplines, including access to a range of external funding opportunities to support businesses and organisations to grow and develop. We can offer you our support to source funding to help boost your company's competitiveness, assist you in exploring innovation needs and to help add value to your business.

In May 2012, the University will open its Enterprise and Innovation Centre (EIC), a landmark initiative which will signal a new approach to university-business engagement. The Centre will bring together all the elements required for successful business growth under one roof – access to markets, finance, technology and skills, as well as traditional business support services.

The EIC will enable university researchers to engage directly with industry and maximise the impact of their research and development activities. It will also provide the infrastructure and resources to enable knowledge transfer and other collaborative project work between the University and external partners, fostering a new approach to "open innovation" within the university environment.

Contact: Dr Barry Timmins,
Head of Business Development
01484 473666
business@hud.ac.uk
www.hud.ac.uk/business

Case study

Small research and development collaboration: Paxman Coolers

Based in Huddersfield, Paxman Coolers' innovative scalp cooling products have been helping to prevent hair loss in chemotherapy patients for over a decade. Keen to increase success rates amongst certain types of chemotherapy patients, the company applied for an "innovation voucher" to fund new research.

The voucher was granted in April this year and since then Paxman Coolers have been working closely with staff and postgraduate students at the University of Huddersfield's Department of Chemical and Biological Sciences to look at the biological process involved in the success of the products. The project involves exposing keratinocyte cells (the most common type of skin cells) to a range of chemotherapy agents whilst being incubated at various temperatures. Because the company chose to work with the University of Huddersfield, it was able to double the amount of funds through the innovation voucher scheme.

Once the research is complete, Paxman Coolers will use the results to improve the efficacy of scalp cooling for patients that are being given those chemotherapy treatments which have previously led to poor scalp cooling results.

Richard Paxman, operations director at the company said: "We are delighted to have been awarded the innovation voucher and certainly would like to explore further work with the University after completion of the first phase. The value added to our business will be excellent, leading to a better understanding of scalp cooling, a better product and treatment and therefore improved efficacy. This will only lead to increased sales throughout the world not only putting Paxman on the map but also our partners".

Knowledge Transfer Partnership: Perrigo

Perrigo, the world's largest manufacturer of OTC (over-the-counter) medicines and healthcare products for private label customers completed a KTP with the University of Huddersfield. The project, based at the company site in Barnsley, led to the successful transformation of paper-based workflow systems into a bespoke, state-of-the-art electronic system, specifically tailored to the stringent requirements of the UK and European pharmaceutical industry. By reducing project materials and increasing software usage the KTP minimised the environmental impact of Perrigo's artwork projects for some years to come. The graduate (or associate) Richard Charnley formally joined Perrigo at the end of the project.

Whatever the nature of the project, KTP involves an exchange of ideas with learning taking place on both sides of the partnership.

Profile

University of Kent

The UK's European university, the University of Kent undertakes innovative world-leading research, and promotes and values innovation, enterprise and creativity in all areas of our activity. Whatever your sector or location, our internationally renowned academics and subject specialists offer a wealth of expertise to develop innovative solutions and give your business the competitive edge.

Expert advice to meet your needs

Here at Kent we provide a wide range of consultancy services to businesses, from supply chain management to the latest electronics design techniques. We will work with you in assessing your requirements quickly and accurately, outlining how our expert advice can benefit your business.

Funding and support for strategic projects

Our innovation voucher scheme gives your business the opportunity to improve growth and performance by tapping into academic knowledge and getting access to specialist facilities and consultancy. Examples include: market research to assist with diversifying into new markets, new software development to assist with the company's growth programme, bespoke training based on the learning requirements within your business, and use of scientific facilities and manpower to assist with a particular process – not only can you draw on the academic knowledge and expertise but use the state of the art facilities for a short or longer-term project.

Business improvement and growth for ambitious owner-managers

From latest research with firms in the south-east, the Centre of Employment, Competitiveness and Growth at Kent has developed "The BIG Journey" programme. Aimed at ambitious owner-managers and directors, with growth potential and who have an inner desire to improve and grow their business, the programme encourages you to work on your business rather than in it, and will challenge you to balance quick wins with longer term business improvement.

Bring new skills and enthusiasm into your organisation

Employing motivated placement students from a wide range of disciplines provides you with a fantastic opportunity to temporarily increase your workforce, complete an innovative project or sample potential graduate employees of the future. Our MBA students can work with your company on tailored projects to assist you with a current business issue or management problem, or be involved in the development of a business case, project development or smart solutions.

Be part of the innovation network

Central to the success of all organisations, ICE: Innovation Creativity Enterprise has evolved from the University of Kent's expertise in working with business and has been shaped by research reports highlighting the role that universities should play in the post-crisis world. ICE is a coherent programme that applies a variety of approaches to engage with companies of all sizes. Members are part of an open innovation network, where like-minded companies collaborate, share ideas and gain easy access to the latest cutting-edge knowledge and innovation. ICE takes a fresh approach to working with businesses that maximises multi-disciplinary working, drawing on the specialist expertise across a whole range of research areas the University offers.

Contact: Carole Barron, Director of Innovation & Enterprise
01227 827376
enterprise@kent.ac.uk
www.icekent.co.uk

Case study

Erlang Solutions Ltd (ES), a niche company specialising in the open source language "Erlang", have doubled their headcount and turnover in the past year. They believe a major reason for this growth and success is the strong working relationship they have with the University of Kent.

The relationship began when ES was invited to perform a guest lecture and student tutorial at the University. Through this initial contact Kent staff were able to see how the company was used to delivering real-world projects, and ES was able to understand what Kent's research ideas were and provide vital feedback on their industrial viability.

Francesco Cesarini, Erlang Solutions Ltd and Professor Simon Thompson, University of Kent, winners of the 2011 University of Kent Innovation Awards

ES developed their first project with the School of Computing at the University. The project team worked to create a new software tool known as "Wrangler", allowing the company to bring solutions to market quickly and cheaply and was funded by the UK-wide Knowledge Transfer Partnerships programme.

So positive was the company's response to working with the University, that they have gone on to collaborate in three further KTPs across Kent Business School, the Unit of Enhancement of Learning and Teaching, School of Computing and School of Engineering and Digital Arts. They have also taken part in two European funded projects and a jointly authored book, *Erlang Programming*, in 2009.

This partnership has allowed ES to be at the forefront of the Erlang based research, and increase its competitiveness while attracting the right employees. In 2009, when most companies were experiencing a reduction in turnover, ES was able to expand by 20% and in 2010 the company doubled in both staff and turnover while maintaining a healthy profit margin. All this was done with their own cashflow, without external investors.

Francesco Cesarini, Erlang Solutions Ltd's founder says: "The projects with the University of Kent have filled knowledge gaps in our organisation, helping us strengthen our position in the market and grow as a company. Our background and skills as a company have been greatly enhanced with the knowledge of the various departments we have interacted with. What has made the projects more exciting, however, is that the knowledge transfer has been flowing in both directions, benefiting the University of Kent. It shows how a small start can lead to an enduring and valuable collaboration, and I encourage other SMEs to try to do the same."

Profile

University of Leeds

Ranked amongst the world's top 100 universities, and the UK's top 10 research universities, with 8,800 staff and over 30,000 students from 130 countries, the University of Leeds is one of the largest employers in the region, contributing £1.23bn a year to the local economy.

Such wide-ranging expertise means we can offer a range of services aimed at encouraging innovation and collaboration with businesses of all sizes and across all sectors.

Enterprising people

We encourage and support enterprising people, and can offer you and your staff a range of professional development opportunities.

Entrepreneurs can join our business school director network for regional SMEs, providing practical and focused learning for SME directors. Alternatively the 10,000 small businesses programme, run in partnership with Goldman Sachs, focuses support on leaders of small businesses and social enterprises to achieve their business growth aspirations.

For larger businesses and organisations we can work with you to develop programmes that address your organisational issues. We offer bespoke education at all levels, ranging from short courses to full degrees. Our programmes are highly interactive, offered on campus or at your workplace, and often lead to recognised qualifications. For example, the flexible format of our Executive MBA means disruption to your work is minimised and you can immerse yourself in the programme away from the workplace.

Our careers centre works successfully with companies who recruit top student and graduate talent to bring new ideas and skills into their business. Leeds graduates are much in demand, so we can offer a free vacancy advertising service, help set up paid internships for students and graduates and can assist you with project definition and short-listing.

From problem solving to expert witness services, development of ideas or products to the provision of independent strategic advice, the world-class research and expertise of Leeds academics can be applied to your business issues, creating solutions that benefit both partners.

Our centres of industrial collaboration (CICs) work in partnership to assist innovative companies, helping them to develop new ideas, materials, products and services.

Knowledge Transfer Partnerships offer your business the opportunity to benefit from specialist expertise, to help find strategic solutions to specific problems. This national scheme enables you to bring a recent graduate into your business, supported by an academic expert, to help solve your particular business challenge.

An enterprising place

Working with us can offer your business a real competitive edge. Since 2006, the University has filed more than 85 patents, incubated over 70 student businesses and spun out 49 innovative new companies. In 2011 we have developed 24 active Knowledge Transfer Partnerships with local, regional and international companies, the seventh highest total in the UK.

0113 343 0900
business@leeds.ac.uk
www.leeds.ac.uk/business

Case study

Historic buildings in need of a facelift may not have to be sand-blasted in future, sparing them from possible surface damage. Researchers from the University of Leeds, working with local company WGL Stoneclean, have shown that an alternative method of industrial cleaning, using diluted acid and super-heated steam, can be used safely on ancient stonework.

The team are now helping Leeds-based SME WGL Stoneclean to convince sceptical clients of the merits of sand-free cleaning. Since commissioning the report, the company's workforce has tripled and its monthly sales have increased tenfold.

The novel "steamacc process" offered by WGL Stoneclean involves spraying blackened stonework with a solution of dilute acid, then washing the surface with a high-pressure jet of super-heated steam at 150 degrees centigrade. The acid essentially opens up the surface of the stone, allowing the steam to penetrate between and behind individual sub-millimetre-sized grains. Deposits of soot and dirt are then forced out by the power of the high pressure wash.

The traditional method of cleaning stonework by shot-blasting the surface with sand, grit or chalk, is effective, but owing to its abrasive nature, can damage the stone grains.

WGL Stoneclean asked civil engineers from the University of Leeds to analyse the surface of stone samples before and after Steamacc cleaning with three different strengths of the dilute acid wash. The researchers used conventional optical microscopy and a high-resolution scanning electron microscope (SEM) to look at samples of stone removed from buildings, and a further set of samples prepared in the laboratory.

Images from the optical microscope confirmed that the process cleaned away the black-grey patina from the weathered York stone effectively. The stone grains themselves were not damaged at all when the acid was used at low concentrations, and only minimal damage was seen at higher concentrations.

Dr Leon Black, of the University of Leeds, who led the study, said: "This is a great demonstration of how academic expertise can be put to good use to help a local business. Our work gave WGL Stoneclean the scientific proof they needed to convince clients that Steamacc cleaning was safe to use and has had a positive impact on their order book."

Bernard Coleman, director of WGL Stoneclean, said: "The figures presented in the report indicate that even if we repeated this cleaning process every five years, it would take 7,000 years to 'wash' a building away. We now believe that the Steamacc process is the least damaging, most cost-effective and environmentally friendly method of cleaning stone buildings that is available in the UK market."

The consultancy work was brokered through Consulting Leeds, the University's dedicated business-facing service, and funded by a voucher scheme run by the government-funded agency Business Link Yorkshire.

Profile

Leeds Metropolitan University

Leeds Metropolitan University is one of the largest universities in the UK with over 30,000 students and nearly 1,000 academic staff. Our University's four faculties (Faculty of Arts, Environment & Technology, Faculty of Business & Law, Faculty of Health & Social Science, and Carnegie Faculty – home to sports, education, languages and events and hospitality) offer businesses a wide range of opportunities to engage with us to enhance and improve their performance.

Leeds Met has developed a range of business engagement options which can be tailored to meet individual needs and budgets.

The Business Enhancement Scheme has been developed to provide opportunities for recently qualified graduates to support businesses over a short intensive period of time. Through this scheme, we can help businesses to make a step change in an area that they have identified as a priority to grow and develop the business. A graduate is employed for eight to 12 weeks to work on the specific project identified. The graduate is employed directly by our university so we take on all recruitment hassles, leaving the business free to concentrate on the improvement issue. In addition to the dedicated employment of the graduate, the business and graduate also receives support from an academic during the timescale of the project. Prices start from just £4,000 plus VAT.

We have a complementary range of products alongside the Business Enhancement Scheme which include the classic KTP, providing businesses with the opportunity to take on a graduate for project work for up to 2 years. Leeds Met has a proven track record for development and delivery of classic KTP – covering areas including: development of governance frameworks; the creation of virtual learning environment content; construction method and knowledge development for restoration projects; and capacity building in manufacturing complemented by guidance on how to restructure a company's activities as a result.

Leeds Met is proud to be a leading provider of professional training and development for the business community. We recognise that high quality, flexible learning is a key factor in allowing professionals to keep up-to-date, remain competent and progress in their careers and we are also able to offer bespoke solutions. We offer professional and executive development, which can be tailored to cater for all business and individual development needs.

Leeds Met also offers products to support start-up and early stage businesses including the QU2 business incubator, business start-up and the innovation showcase.

To discuss any of the above options or to take advantage of a free diagnostic consultation with one of our business development managers please contact the University's Enterprise Office.

0113 812 1904
enterprise@leedsmet.ac.uk
www.leedsmet.ac.uk/business

Case study

Leeds Metropolitan University has supported a number of successful Knowledge Transfer Partnerships over the last three decades. The following is a case study of a recent KTP with Vacform Group (Yorkshire) Ltd.

Vacform Group (Yorkshire) Limited is a family run business, established in 1967, which produces thermo-plastic mouldings by vacuum forming for component assembly, fabrication, design, pattern making and mould services for a wide variety of products.

The company currently employs 34 staff and has branches in Leeds and Chesterfield. In order to improve its client service and reduce reliance on subcontractors, the company decided that they wished to participate in a Knowledge Transfer Partnership (KTP) to introduce a tooling division (capable of producing tooling and prototypes) to create opportunities for future growth. The organisation wanted to produce its own tools in-house and provide design services thus giving more control to the company and ensuring a quick turnaround for clients (both existing and new) in terms of receiving quotes, tools and orders.

Working with academics from Leeds Metropolitan University's Innovation North Faculty, the KTP associate (Mustafa El-Etriby) was employed for a two-year period to take this project forward.

The tooling division, which commenced operation in April 2007, was created as a stand-alone company (the Vacform Group (Tooling) Ltd) with the intention that this organisation would supply all the company's sites and the wider industry. As well as running this new company, the KTP associate introduced new technology and software into the Group. This new capability has also allowed the company to develop its own new products and market streams.

At the end of the project, the tooling division was a fully functioning and profit enhancing part of the Group and Mustafa accepted a permanent role within the organisation. The university maintains its links with the company and both institutions are exploring opportunities for further collaboration.

For more information see www.vac-form.com/index.html.

Profile

University of Liverpool

As one of the UK's top research-led, Russell Group universities, the University of Liverpool has a long track record of working in partnership with a wide range of organisations – nationally and internationally. Through partnership with the university and by accessing our research knowledge, skills and expertise, partners have been able to tackle head on the real-life issues facing their organisations; transforming ideas into creative solutions, new technologies, strategies, policies, applications, products or skills.

Organisations who've already engaged with the University of Liverpool have benefited from the following.

- New skills, insights and innovative thinking.
- Improved business performance with increased cost-effectiveness and profitability.
- More efficient processes and systems.
- New product development or improvements.
- Advanced technologies and techniques with industrial application.
- Competitive advantage, growth and strategic change.

How to access our expertise

There are numerous ways for organisations to access and benefit from our research expertise.

- Research programmes.
- Knowledge Transfer Partnerships (KTPs).
- State of the art facilities and equipment.
- Consultancy.
- Continuing professional development (CPD).
- Student projects and placements.
- Intellectual property (IP).
- Postgraduate studentships, PhDs.

Other services include: feedback and analysis of data, testing/trial new products, support with regulatory issues, help with applying for research grants and funding opportunities, developing innovative ways of connecting with the public.

The University's Business Gateway is dedicated to providing advice and assistance to organisations interested in developing a relationship with the University of Liverpool. An experienced team of business managers work closely with organisations to gain a specific understanding of needs and works at the interface with the University's academic community to create innovative, often multi-disciplinary solutions that work.

A MEMBER OF THE RUSSELL GROUP

0845 0700 064
business@liverpool.ac.uk
www.liverpool.ac.uk/
businessgateway

Case study

Genlec, part of the Energetix Group, specialises in low carbon and clean energy technology. It has developed a micro-combined heat and power (mCHP) technology for the domestic heating market.

A Knowledge Transfer Partnership (KTP) with the University of Liverpool helped Genlec to improve the efficiency and performance of its core technology at an accelerated rate, reducing development times and dramatically improving the quality of the designs produced. It also enabled the company to enter the market place at an earlier point and with a reduced development cost.

KTPs enable businesses with a strategic need to access the university's expertise to improve their competitiveness, productivity and performance. The scheme, funded by the Technology Strategy Board, involves a high calibre graduate working in a company with academic supervision. This often results in strategic advantages for the company, academic benefits to the university and valuable experience to the graduate.

The partnership with Genlec improved their understanding of thermodynamics and heat transfer processes, creating additional competency for the business in these areas. As an energy technology company, Genlec will reap the benefits of this across a range of areas, from enhanced product quality and performance, to opening up new markets.

The KTP also resulted in the filing of two patents which will significantly strengthen Genlec's competitive position. This additional intellectual property complements the company's core organic Rankine cycle patent, providing subsystem and component level protection.

The results of the KTP are as follows.

- The direct contribution of the KTP to the sales of the product is estimated to be worth £1.5m.

- Improved efficiency and performance has resulted in reduced development costs.

- A dramatic reduction in the amount of time required to design and test steam circuits.

- Competitive position improved through additional intellectual property.

Find out more about Knowledge Transfer Partnerships at www.liv.ac.uk/ktp.

This project has been of great benefit to Energetix Genlec, delivering tangible strategic advantages whilst strengthening our links with a leading academic research base.

Profile

London South Bank University

At London South Bank University (LSBU) we understand that getting on with business is ultimately about getting on. Getting on with business means meeting new challenges, never being satisfied and always pushing forward. At LSBU we recognise that businesses need the reassurance of technical excellence and thoughtful, practical solutions that provide great results every time.

We have extensive experience of supporting organisations across a wide range of sectors. Whether you need training, research, knowledge transfer or consultancy services, our focus is on getting the results to help your business grow.

Knowledge transfer
Knowledge transfer is about accessing university expertise for the benefit of industry and is designed to help improve competitiveness and productivity. At the heart of every partnership is a two to three-year project designed to meet the specific strategic objectives of an organisation, a high quality graduate plus hands-on support from LSBU's academic experts. LSBU runs a wide variety of knowledge transfer projects and has collaborated with over 100 companies.

Research and consultancy
New and innovative thinking is vital for organisations to remain competitive. Working with LSBU gives you access to academics and experts trained to challenge existing ways of thinking and find novel solutions. Sometimes all that an organisation needs is a fresh perspective and we can offer that to you through a short term consultancy or research project or through a longer term partnership. We can support how your business operates, evaluate your processes and develop, design and test new systems, services and products.

Bespoke training and CPD
Drawing on our wide ranging expertise, we offer a selection of training courses, conferences and events to meet the needs of business. Our courses can be tailored to meet both the specific needs of your organisation and the individual requirements of your staff, enabling you to improve productivity and address skills gaps.

Our cross-faculty themes promote internal as well as external collaboration and mean we are well equipped to provide solutions to organisations from all sectors. Our areas of excellence are:

- delivering health and well-being

- engineering a cleaner, energy-efficient future

- innovation through creativity and design

- building a sustainable urban environment

- addressing society's challenges – today and beyond.

The Research and Business
Development Office
020 7815 6923
gettingon@lsbu.ac.uk
www.lsbu.ac.uk/business

Case study

Cleaner air for London: running London's greenest taxis on chip fat

Simon Hughes, Bermondsey and Old Southwark MP, now runs his yellow Hackney carriage on used restaurant vegetable oil thanks to Central London's only biodiesel producer, Uptown Biodiesel.

Uptown Biodiesel are setting a precedent for green transport by collecting used vegetable oil from London's restaurants and turning it into carbon neutral, environmentally friendly biodiesel that is fuelling green taxis all over London.

Based under the railway arches in Southwark, the company didn't need to look far to get the academic validation they needed to prove the quality of their fuel to their clients. LSBU's chemical engineer Imad Al-Wahaib and mechanical and manufacturing engineer, Abdullah Ajmal, recognised that the company's oil did not meet the European standards and so devised a way to not only increase the quality of their fuel but also to develop the mechanical handling process which has previously involved manually filtering a five gallon tub of oil. "Within a couple of months the company managed to get from an 85% pure product to a 95% pure product, an amazing achievement," reports Tony Day, professor of energy engineering at LSBU.

Nigel Jewison, managing director says: "I have always been a great believer in education and training. Working with top professors at London South Bank University has given us a real opportunity to expand our knowledge whilst simultaneously pushing the company towards new levels of success."

Conversion rates of fuel have improved considerably meaning the company is now in a position to supply their biodiesel to global giants such as PricewaterhouseCoopers (PwC). In fact Uptown Biodiesel have been contracted to supply PwC at London Bridge a massive 45,000 litres of recycled fuel per month to power the generator at their new offices.

Uptown Biodiesel are now leaders in their field and have room to upscale their activities thanks to this successful partnership. "We are looking forward to working together again in the very near future on other projects," says Nigel.

Profile

Manchester Metropolitan University

The university for world-class professionals

Manchester Metropolitan University's (MMU) dedicated research and
enterprise services team helps business to unlock the benefits of working
with a major university. At MMU we have the expertise and experience to help our partners
to overcome business challenges and to access resources that will enable them to grow.

Solutions for business

Whether it's professionally oriented and accredited courses or applied research and consultancy
– our sector-specific business development managers will work with you to design and deliver
solutions that reflect the needs of your organisation.

We deliver:

- corporate training programmes including bespoke short courses
- consultancy and research development
- Knowledge Transfer Partnerships
- student projects including placements.

Clients range from the global to the local including: Tesco, Goldman Sachs, HMRC, Rolls-Royce, IBM,
Marks & Spencer... and literally hundreds of SMEs.

Robin Wilson, director of PR and social media at McCann Manchester says: "MMU remains fantastic
at producing our digital talent of the future. The award-winning programme we have jointly
developed equips our new staff with comprehensive knowledge and practical skills that businesses
need to grow in this digital and social age."

Early stage incubation and SME support

MMU has particular expertise in servicing the needs of start-ups through Innospace, our business
incubation hub located in central Manchester. Innospace offers pre-incubation and start-up support
at unbelievable rates to over 120 SMEs. Many of Innospace's tenants are in high-growth sectors such
as the creative and digital industries and professional and business services. Innospace is expanding
so if you want to access a growing community of switched-on innovators and entrepreneurs then go
to: www.innospace.co.uk for contact details.

Bruce Thomas, director of Modern English, a social media agency whose clients include EMI, BBC,
AstraZeneca and Warner Music, says: "Since moving into Innospace our business has grown financially
and just as important, the vibrant culture means we are all really looking forward to going to work."

Regional in focus, international in impact

MMU's status as the second largest university in the UK means that our expertise spans a wide
variety of industries – many of which are critical to the development of the local economy such
as creative and digital media, food and tourism, retail, health
and wellbeing, urban education and SMEs in general. Over
the last five years MMU has helped north-west companies to
safeguard over 450 jobs, increase sales by £44m and develop
over 200 new products and processes.

Research and Enterprise Services
Contact: Andy Chance-Hill
0161 247 1032
a.chance-hill@mmu.ac.uk
www.mmu.ac.uk/business

Case study

Win-Win: how Manchester Met helped a local bakery to develop a £12m turnover

Knowledge Transfer Partnerships rarely work better than the lasting alliance between MMU and the Wrexham-based Village Bakery. When managing director Robin Jones approached MMU in 2007, he wanted help to develop a gluten-free range for his business, and in a very short space of time the new division has grown its turnover to £12m. Village Bakery Nutrition is now the largest gluten-free bakery in Europe, using a £3m facility to manufacture 2,500 loaves an hour.

Robin Jones, Managing Director of the Village Bakery says: "We worked with the University in 2001 and they had a strong academic team so when we started up this place in 2008 we thought they were the natural partner to work with, because of their expertise in coeliac, the disease suffered by people who need gluten free. We like working with MMU because they have fantastic academic staff, great resources and the team we work with is excellent. It's easy for me to talk to the University and put into place exactly what I need."

Raphael Cabrera was installed as part of the KTP scheme and he quickly set about the task of familiarising himself with the bakery and training staff, before applying his expertise to expanding the company's product range. In the last two years, Cabrera has helped launch a new pizza range as well as seven different types of loaf. Staff numbers in the division have doubled to 45 in line with turnover and profit.

Both MMU and the Village Bakery understand the importance of innovation to the strength of the business. Dr Valentine Stojceska, the University's academic partner says: "We had to advise the company on how to improve the products by using the laboratory equipment at MMU and testing exhaustively. We offered our expertise and our facilities because the company didn't have the equipment on site in Wrexham."

The KTP is finished and Cabrera is now fully employed by the company – always one of the best ways of measuring the success of a KTP. The partnership between MMU and the Village Bakery will not stop there, however, as Robin Jones already has other ideas: "We have another bakery next door and are speaking with the team at the University to try to find funding for another KTP placement. We want to ensure that as the Village Bakery grows, so does our knowledge base, and I'd like the university to be part of that growth as it has been over the past few years."

Profile

Newcastle University

Part of the elite Russell Group of UK universities, Newcastle University Business School is an ambitious, forward-thinking institution born out of one of the UK's most reputable, research-intensive universities. Global accreditations from EQUIS and AMBA are testament to the school's high quality research, teaching and industry engagement.

The Business School plays an important role in the University's "Vision 2021" strategy and aims to be a top 20 European business school by 2014. It has a renewed focus on national and international industry partnerships that connect students to employers, influence policy and practice, and ensure "real-world" relevance to the academic product.

Employability and entrepreneurship have been key elements within the Business School's culture for many years; as such its graduate employment rates are extremely high, as are the number of students wishing to establish their own companies. Aside from one of the best university careers services in the UK, the Business School has developed successful models for global work placements and internships that benefit both employers and students, and ensure that the student experience has international opportunity at its core.

The Business School has grown exponentially since its formal inception in 2002: with 2,800 students, it currently accounts for 17% of Newcastle University's undergraduate population. Since 2008, student numbers have risen by 40%, thanks to the increasing popularity of Newcastle as a place to study at both undergraduate and postgraduate levels. Today, students from 70 countries are represented across a diverse suite of academic, industry-relevant programmes that make it more than "just another management school".

This growth has financed a £50m, state-of-the-art headquarters, opened in July 2011, in the heart of the city. Next door to this iconic building is St James' Park, one of the UK's biggest and most exciting sporting destinations, attracting tens of thousands of football fans to every Newcastle United home game.

Newcastle is renowned as one of the best university cities in the UK. Its friendly people, low-cost living, and vibrant cultural and entertainment scene are attributes the Geordie people are very proud of, and appeal to students from all walks of life. The European Commission rates Newcastle as one of the top three cities in Europe for quality of life. These assets, combined with a compelling story of growth and investment, have attracted outstanding academic talent from around the world to the Business School, talent that is evident in the classroom, out in the international business community, and in the faculty's research activity.

Dr Joanna Berry
joanna.berry@ncl.ac.uk
0191 208 1500
www.ncl.ac.uk/nubs

Case study

Natural Empathy: a case study in engagement

Natural Empathy gets "second solution" for marketing

Northumberland-based ethical and natural beauty brand, Natural Empathy, invited student teams from Newcastle University Business School to check the validity of its marketing idea for selling direct to customers. One of the teams was tasked with developing the company's original idea while a second team looked for an alternative execution of that idea. This approach ties in with a creative technique called "second solution". It involves trying to get a second right answer to a problem, the theory being that, more often than not, a second solution will actually be better than the first solution.

Brainpower

To make sure nothing was overlooked, a third team of students considered completely different marketing ideas for the company's natural beauty products (possibly a "third solution"!). Each team comprised up to eight students, so there was a lot of combined brainpower and energy being applied to the project. Philip Stuckey, Strategic Director for Natural Empathy, said: "Originally we were thinking of having demonstrators talk at 'parties' in people's homes about our products and their organic ingredients. The main issue was that people might feel pressured to buy if a demonstrator were present. Also, recruiting demonstrators could have been a problem for us."

Initiative

To generate fresh ideas, the students initiated focus groups with their friends and canvassed opinion at the Metro Centre. Philip says, "They came up with the idea of 'virtual' demonstration methods that avoided any pressure and solved our recruitment problem, too. A bonus idea was to add luxury products from other suppliers to make a party more interesting and fun." He continues: "The marketing students really surpassed our expectations with their insight and strategic thinking. We decided to adopt one of the group's solutions, and we were also able to add the best ideas from the other groups. It's certainly been rewarding to work with Newcastle University Business School and we have already done it again."

Profile

Norwich University College of the Arts

ideas factory@NUCA

Since 1845 Norwich University College of the Arts (NUCA) has provided higher education in the arts, design and media. There has always been a strong tradition of collaborative projects with companies that are looking for innovative thinking, which continues to this day.

As a specialist institution, NUCA promotes the importance of creativity for business and encourages entrepreneurship and ideas-based thinking. Students are encouraged to demonstrate the rationale behind their work and must always state why it is as it is.

In 2010, ideas factory@NUCA was established to formalise links between businesses and NUCA and to provide a single point of entry for those wishing to work with NUCA. Business processes have been put in place to provide excellent client service while further fostering unique creative thinking.

ideas factory@NUCA draws on our staff and students' ideas and expertise and undertakes consultancy, projects and commissions for businesses and other external clients. Students work in teams to address business problems and offer creative solutions. This provides a platform for exceptional new thinking and fresh ideas. Students are supported by academic staff and technicians, many of whom have experience of working in the creative industries.

Examples of external commercial work undertaken include brand identity, naming, web design, product design, publishing design, packaging, advertising and art commissions for commercial and private clients. Also, NUCA hold prestigious Apple iOS developer status, such that we can develop apps for iPhone and iPad.

When it comes to design, style, taste and trend forecasting, our students are knowledgeable, discerning and articulate, and ideas factory@NUCA also offers opportunities to engage students in market research. Hence clients get access to the ideas of the new generation of creative thinkers and consumers, whilst our students gain experience of real work contexts and environments.

However, don't just take our word for it. The *Guardian* recently ranked NUCA as the best specialist institution for art and design in England and our clients say the following: "The campaign leaflets and posters reflected our brand perfectly and were both sensitive and challenging of age stereotypes. Feedback from stakeholders including the press has been very positive", Suzanne Handsley, head of corporate and individual giving, Age UK Norfolk.

"Once again our congratulations on the excellent work", says David Smith, IT manager, Start-rite Shoes Ltd. "Working with ideas factory@NUCA on this project has enabled us to tap into a wealth of creative talent at a very local level. Our board was both impressed and delighted with the concepts you presented and we are now looking forward to taking your ideas out to our staff. A big thank you to you and your team," says David McQuade, chief executive, Flagship Housing Group.

ideas factory@NUCA
01603 610561
ideasfactory@NUCA.ac.uk
www.NUCA.ac.uk/ideasfactory

Case study

Archant is the one of the UK's leading regional media businesses, owning websites and publishing magazines and daily and weekly newspapers including the *Eastern Daily Press* and *Norwich Evening News*. Small, classified adverts are still a strong revenue stream, but were described as "unloved".

Brief

- To re-imagine the classifieds section.
- To create a cleaner contemporary style that would unify the look of all the classifieds sections across the company.
- To develop iconography to categorise and highlight sections.
- To develop information graphics to highlight pricing and readership figures.
- Finally, to create an attractive and appealing advertising campaign which would highlight the re-launch of the classifieds advertising format.

Solution

Students and academics at ideas factory@NUCA began working together. A consultancy session deemed the terminology old fashioned and out of touch with modern online auction sites. A new name "SMALL ADS" was proposed. The team designed layouts of the relevant sections: "births, marriages and deaths", "retail" and "public announcements". They went on to design iconography, before producing a style guide to enable implementation by Archant's in-house production team.

ideas factory@NUCA also developed a press advertising campaign, which highlighted the eclectic offer of goods, services and announcements. Using a hand-drawn typographic style, these offers were spread across the page in a variety of colours. The final creative is flexible enough to allow a number of adverts, each reflecting the redesigned SMALL ADS section and announcing its confident re-launch to a younger demographic.

Results

Following a trial launch in the *Norwich Advertiser*, the SMALL ADS format has now been launched in the *Eastern Daily Press* and the *Norwich Evening News*. The *Norwich Advertiser* has seen revenue increase 26% since re-design, and inbound calls regarding SMALL ADS in the *Eastern Daily Press* and *Norwich Evening News* have increased by 8%.

Client quote

Adrian Jeakings, chief executive, Archant says: "Archant is one of the UK's largest independently owned regional media businesses. We were delighted to be involved at an early stage in discussions about the University College's ideas factory@NUCA initiative, and to provide a number of pilot projects. These were successfully delivered by NUCA staff and students and Archant has continued to commission designs and other creative projects from ideas factory@NUCA.

"The quality of work produced by NUCA is exemplary. In particular, we at Archant have been impressed and delighted by students' creative thinking and problem-solving and their highly original design solutions. Our relationship with ideas factory@NUCA has brought unexpected benefits; for example, invigorating debate about the Archant brand and creating employment opportunities for students on graduation. We believe that the University College's approach to employer engagement, as demonstrated by ideas factory@NUCA, demonstrates an institution which is thinking creatively and acting positively to build external relationships and to support the local and regional economy."

Profile

University of Nottingham

UNITED KINGDOM · CHINA · MALAYSIA

The University of Nottingham is one of the world's leading universities: a trailblazer for globalisation in higher education; the third most popular UK university by undergraduate applications; and Britain's seventh best university for 'research power', strengthened by knowledge transfer and entrepreneurship.

Research power and innovation creating impact

As one of Britain's most successful research-intensive universities, Nottingham's research delivers real benefits to society and the economy. The University of Nottingham climbed seven places in seven years (more than any other university) to join the top seven institutions in the 2008 Research Assessment Exercise (RAE), reflecting research excellence, breadth and depth.

The University's total research portfolio is worth over £300m. This funds more than 2,300 research projects. The University attracts more research funding, over £150m last year, than most other universities. It also has more than 200 industrial sponsors of research, all part of research enterprises that seek to make global impact.

Nobel Prize-winning research has revolutionised medical diagnostics in the past 30 years thanks to Professor Sir Peter Mansfield's research at Nottingham into magnetic resonance imaging and development of MRI scans. Pioneering cochlear implantation programmes for deaf children, transgenic tomatoes, safer pedestrian crossings, drug discovery and regenerative medicine breakthroughs all began here.

Creating innovative business opportunities

Professor Chris Rudd, Pro-Vice-Chancellor for Knowledge Transfer and Business Engagement, oversees Nottingham's strategy for ensuring its world-changing research is successfully commercialised, contributing to the economic success of the East Midlands and the UK.

He is responsible for Business Engagement and Innovation Services, including the Technology Transfer Office, which manages a portfolio of over 300 patents and supports licensing of university inventions and forming and growing new spin-out companies. "The University of Nottingham has a very strong track record transforming brilliant discoveries and research insights from concepts into new products and processes," said Professor Rudd.

Business engagement activities include: consultancy; licensing of intellectual property; knowledge transfer partnerships; knowledge transfer secondments; services-rendered projects – for example the Advanced Manufacturing Unit, the Environment Technology Centre, the Medical Engineering Unit, and the Chemical Innovation Laboratory; CASE studentships; student placements; internships; and research programmes structured to support businesses.

In 2008, The University of Nottingham became the first *Times Higher Education* 'Entrepreneurial University of the Year', because its training, support and encouragement enable academics and students to create enterprises. Judges said the University was "committed to nurturing the most enterprising and globally-minded graduates in British higher education". The accolade followed a Queen's Award for Innovation, presented to the University's School of Pharmacy in 2007.

General enquiries
Paul Hamley
paul.hamley@nottingham.ac.uk
0115 951 5743

Case study

Nottingham's catalyst for chemistry and enterprise

What links inorganic nanoparticles for high-tech engineering applications, and supercritical fluid technologies for drug discovery and development, with "bagpipe oil" and glue for cows? They represent some of the many business engagement success stories managed by the Business Partnership Unit (BPU) within the School of Chemistry at The University of Nottingham.

This BPU approach, led by Dr Trevor Farren, has helped gain the School of Chemistry a distinctive reputation across the chemistry-using business sector for developing innovative solutions to industry problems. Trevor and his team of Business Science Fellows (BSFs) encourage entrepreneurial activities, support collaborations and offer specialist services to large and small businesses. This strengthens vital links with business and adds value across research and teaching activity.

"Key to BPU's success is its full integration within the school and having sector specific skills and expertise that are targeted at the needs of chemistry-using businesses," said Trevor, a polymer chemist and a former senior manager with Courtaulds plc.

"With input from industry, we have created a range of entrepreneurial training courses. These include our BSF programme that enables postdoctoral scientists to work within the BPU on a range of business related projects allowing them to develop business skills while advancing the schools technology transfer and business engagement portfolio. I have seen a much more business-aware culture develop here in since we set up the BPU in 2000."

The team has a huge network of links with chemistry using businesses and is a focal point for enquiries, matching company needs with the School's capabilities. BSFs such as Dr Freya Hine and Dr Katherine Scovell manage relationships with industry partners and oversee shorter term feasibility studies and technology transfer projects.

"With support from the EU through the European Regional Development Fund, we recently initiated a project that allows us to meet the needs of SMEs even more effectively," said Dr Hine. "Qualifying businesses now benefit from free initial access to high-level skills, specialist facilities and new technologies to help them tackle challenges, innovate and grow."

The BPU's extensive alumni network also benefits industry. Over 20 BSFs have been trained in the past decade and former BSFs now have very interesting career paths. Leading research and consulting company Oakdene Hollins Ltd, which promotes more sustainable and less carbon-intensive products, processes and services, has recruited two former BSFs as consultants.

"Previously, we would not have considered appointing young post-doctoral researchers direct from university without relevant industry experience," said Nick Morley, a founding director of the firm. "The experience these individuals gained from working in Nottingham's School of Chemistry Business Partnership Unit means they're ideally suited to working with business, industry and policy-makers in the ways in which we do."

Profile

Plymouth University

Plymouth University engages with organisations of all sizes but we particularly recognise the importance of smaller companies in the region so work to actively support them with their development.

At a regional level, excellent groundwork to establish and embed the Growth Acceleration and Investment Network (GAIN) is pulling together over £100m of assets – including Tamar Science Park and the business pre-incubation facilities on our campus – to create what we've termed an "innovation ecosystem". It brings together businesses, investors, researchers and academia into a network that will support the development and growth of enterprise across the peninsula. Just some of the unique components of GAIN will be the University's new £20m marine building (opening in 2012) and the installation of a state of the art electron microscope, housed in a dedicated centre. These facilities will provide testing arenas, technology and specialist incubation space for the marine and renewable energy and composites sectors, which offer so much potential for the region.

GAIN establishes "an umbrella", co-ordinating other important facets of the ecosystem, such as the ERDF-supported innovation centres in Cornwall. The University operates these on behalf of Cornwall Council, and established the first at Pool. The second at Tremough is due to open in January 2012 and we have signed the management agreement to operate a third in January 2013. Combined, these centres will accommodate over 150 businesses, employing some 600 people by 2015.

But GAIN is much more than physical assets; it provides businesses with access to academics and researchers and, importantly, it can connect them with some of the money needed to make their ideas happen. The University manages the first project funded through Government's Regional Growth Fund – the Plymouth University & Western Morning News Growth Fund – providing £1m in grants direct to small and medium-sized businesses. And we have already run the first of what will be a series of investor days, lining up serious investors to look at the boldest business ideas from the region. And when these ideas look like taking off, GAIN provides businesses with expert advice on how to protect their intellectual property through a contract with Frontier IP.

On campus, we provide a varied portfolio of support: free monthly sessions for entrepreneurs to pitch their ideas to a panel of experts, the annual "business ideas challenge" with support and cash prizes for the winners, and workshops providing the skills and knowledge required to turn ideas into viable businesses. Through our Enterprise Solutions Service we also broker access to leading academics, students and graduates, higher level skills and facilities: we are "open for business".

This year we worked with over 2,500 businesses, including through our award-winning Knowledge Transfer Partnerships and graduate internships: which created over 270 internships; more than any other in the region. Through the allocation of economic challenge investment fund money, we helped 1,900 individuals and 950 businesses, awarding £420,000 of enterprise vouchers to pay for CPD, careers support and access to our services and facilities.

Enterprise Solutions
0800 052 5600
enterprisesolutions@plymouth.ac.uk
www.plymouth.ac.uk/enterprisesolutions

Case study

Fosi Originals launches innovative ski safety wear

Fosi creator Barbara Lees has been skiing since she was a teenager and has also run several successful businesses including a ski accommodation business in Austria. Dissatisfied with how she looked in a ski helmet and recognising that this was a common problem, Barbara set about customising her helmet to be more aesthetically pleasing and hence, the Fosi collection was born.

The Fosi is a simple aesthetic band that fits around any ski helmet to create a glamorous and fashionable look. It is interchangeable and doesn't cover the whole helmet so the vents are clear, with no adverse effect on the safety or functionality.

Barbara contacted the University's enterprise solutions team for assistance and was able to obtain funding through enterprise vouchers enabling her to rent space in Formation 2.0, one of the University's business start-up pre-incubation spaces. The team were also able to put her in touch with recent graduate Verity Cole via the University's graduate internship programme and facilitate access to academic expertise in translational languages and marketing.

The opportunity to access additional resources and centrally located office space allowed Barbara to concentrate on driving her business forward, resulting in national press coverage and a boom in sales. Barbara's business success has also been recognised in the University's annual business ideas challenge 2010–2011 where she was awarded the second prize. She said: "The university's incubation space has provided a low-cost platform from which to launch our new business. We are grateful for the access to expertise and additional resources, which have allowed us to really focus the project and successfully launch the new products in time for the British Ski and Board Show. Since the launch, we have been overwhelmed by the response to Fosi and were thrilled to be featured as one of the hottest new ski products in the *Daily Mail* newspaper. The supportive and collaborative working environment at Plymouth University is a great start for any new business."

For Verity, the chance to work in a new business has been a great opportunity to learn about product and brand development. She said: "Being involved in a small business through the internship programme at an early stage in product and brand development has been an exciting journey. I believe the quality of experience and level of support that I have received would be difficult to match in a larger organisation."

Profile

University of Salford

The University of Salford has always had a business focus, especially when it comes to Knowledge Transfer Partnerships.

KTP is one of Europe's leading programmes combining graduate recruitment with knowledge exchange. The benefit of KTP is proven across a range of measures, whether it be company development and profitability, knowledge exchange between universities and business, or job creation. Knowledge Transfer Partnerships programme is intentionally flexible in its delivery, allowing projects to vary in length from 12 to 36 months, and the knowledge base partners eligible to participate.

Funded by the Technology Strategy Board along with the other government funding organisations, KTPs are collaborations between academics; a company that needs their expertise and a graduate (Associate) recruited to work on a project central to the requirements of the business and its development.

By participating in a Knowledge Transfer Partnership, businesses and organisations can:

- access up to 67% grant funding
- access expertise and innovative solutions to help your business grow
- receive help with the development of new and pioneering technologies
- improve your organisation's operational efficiency
- benefit from an increase of over £270,000 in annual profits before tax
- create three genuine new jobs.

Academics can:

- identify new research themes and undergraduate/postgraduate projects
- apply knowledge and expertise to important business problems
- develop business relevant teaching and research material
- contribute to the Research Excellence Framework
- publish high quality research papers
- help businesses and organisations improve their competitiveness and productivity.

Associate can:

- enhance their career prospects by being provided with the opportunity to manage a challenging project central to a company's strategic development and long-term growth
- receive top class training and development in management and leadership skills
- benefit from an excellent chance of permanent employment at the end of the KTP (75% of Associates are offered employment on completion of their project, and overall 59% accept).

If you feel that your business or organisation could benefit from the University's expertise, please contact us on the number below.

Contact: Janet Morana,
Partnerships Manager
0161 295 2902
j.morana@salford.ac.uk
www.ktp.salford.ac.uk

Case study

With a client list including Manchester United, Heineken, Scholl, Nike, Mölnlycke Health Care and Kumho Tyres, the Foundry has won numerous international industry awards including the New York festivals innovative advertising award and world design medals.

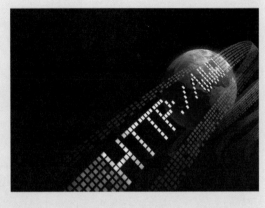

Working alongside so many multinational clients the Foundry realised that each company had many agencies in different countries, each creating similar projects but each with their own overhead and charges. They then identified a gap in the market for a software application that would allow multinationals to design their own POS (point-of-sale) materials and make them available, via the internet, to their customers, who could then tailor and print them as needed in any language anywhere in the world thus giving huge return on an investment of agency fees. And so the POS store came to pass.

The Foundry began the process of creating such a system, however the skill set to develop the software to the required level did not currently exist within the workforce. One option was to employ someone with the software skill set, but as the project was in its embryonic stage this was a difficult investment to make. During an ad hoc conversation with the DTi the Foundry were introduced to the Knowledge Transfer Partnership programme. The KTP programme offered the ideal solution, benefiting both parties and creating job opportunities. It became apparent during discussions that alongside the development of the project, the Foundry would also benefit from the internal learning and up-skilling of its staff alongside the KTP associate. This would ensure that future information and system developments within the company were scalable, maintainable, robust and not dependent on one person.

John Muirhead, KTP associate, said: "I was really chuffed to be given the opportunity to develop such a novel piece of software", but as he later discovered he has also been given the opportunity to develop himself in many other ways. John continued: "The key challenge was to develop a piece of packaged software that could be easily reconfigured for use by different brand owners to support the delivery of their specific point-of-sale materials and ancillary items to their customer base. That meant it had to be generic enough to allow multiple reconfigurations to support radically different brands."

The working relationship between the Foundry and KTP has been a great success. Kevin Murphy, managing director, says: "Working alongside the guys from the KTP has been an absolute joy. They have understood our business needs and have helped John and ourselves every step of the way. For us it has been the perfect partnership."

Profile

University of Southampton

UNIVERSITY OF
Southampton

The University of Southampton is "open for business" and tailors its services and facilities to industry demand, providing flexible mechanisms for collaboration, ranging from half a day's consultancy or facility hire to long-term strategic research relationships. The University is a proven partner of choice for industry, the public and third sectors and has a strong track record of working with small and medium-sized enterprises (SMEs). It has been ranked as one of the top UK universities for working with SME partners, and receiving SME income, as recorded in the University sector's standard annual return (£10.3m in 2009–10). The University also has long-term relationships with global corporations including Airbus, Rolls-Royce, Microsoft, IBM, Lloyd's Register and Phillips.

The University has developed a flexible approach to collaboration with a number of schemes open to companies, from student projects and placements through consultancy and secondments to sponsored research projects as well the government flagship scheme – Knowledge Transfer Partnerships (KTP). The University has a strong portfolio of KTP programmes which draw on the University's excellent research base, bringing benefits to all parties. In 2011 two of these partnerships attracted regional and national awards.

In addition to building strength in industrial collaboration, the University of Southampton is a leading creator of spin-out companies, developing its own business incubator which provides specialist business development support and facilities for high-tech start-up companies.

Southampton has been placed in the top three universities worldwide for the quality of its spin-out companies. Thirteen successful companies have been spun out from Southampton since 2000, four of which have been floated on London's Alternative Investment Market (AIM) with a combined market capitalisation value of £180 million. These companies have been built on the back of a number of great University of Southampton technologies which have transformed society, including the following.

- Optical fibres technology now used as *the* communications platform, originally created by our Optoelectronics Research Centre.

- The open-source data project in electronics and computer science, which has led to the integration of complex government data sets.

- Quieter aircraft engines developed by our world-leading Institute of Sound and Vibration Research.

- Olympic gold medal winning sporting technology deployed by Amy Williams in the Bob Skeleton event at the winter Olympics and the cycling team in the Beijing Olympics developed by academics in engineering sciences.

Tapping into the University's knowledge can help companies develop innovative products and services as well as efficient processes and procedures – all of which can help them gain the competitive edge.

023 8059 3095
ris@southampton.ac.uk
www.soton.ac.uk/business

Case study

Structural Metal Decks Ltd (SMD), based in Poole, Dorset, is an SME engaged in the design, supply and installation of composite metal decking and accessories to the construction industry. In 2009 they approached the University of Southampton's Faculty of Engineering and the Environment in order to redesign a new range of trapezoidal profiles to reaffirm SMD as one of the UK's leading providers of structural decking systems. The result was a highly successful, two-year KTP project sponsored by the Technology Strategy Board.

SMD Ltd's existing profiles are being used in the lower floors of the Shard building in London (Europe's tallest building). The new profiles, developed within this highly successful KTP, will be used on floors 74–81; the first time they have been used at these levels. "It is incredibly exciting to witness the impact of our research such a short time after its completion," stated Dr Boyd, lead academic on the KTP.

Dr Bloodworth, the academic supervisor on this project, oversaw the experimental testing and said it was "highly beneficial to the University's laboratory to be involved in the Eurocode Building Standards testing of these new profiles, especially as the laboratory undertook the testing of the original SMD Ltd profiles in the 1980s".

The research associate employed on the project, Wai Yuk Lau, was supported by the University in the development of numerical modelling methodologies to allow the virtualisation of the performance of future concept profiles. This approach negates time-consuming and expensive testing at the initial concept design stage. Supervised by Dr Boyd, the project utilised the world-leading computational modelling capability at the University.

Jamie Turner, technical director at SMD Ltd, commented: "The use of finite element analysis in the development of future concept profiles is an incredible opportunity that would not have been possible without this KTP relationship with the University of Southampton. It provides us with the methods required to maintain and improve our market position once the deep national recession that has hit the civil engineering industry lifts."

SMD as a company do not have an in-house R&D department. The KTP gave the company the knowledge and tools to enable the concept stage of future R&D to be carried out in-house and provided links with the University for future testing requirements.

The knowledge embedded during the project has given the company the ability to disseminate this knowledge to the wider industry. This will prove to be of great benefit in opening up new collaborations, and has already realised new international contracts for the company.

Profile

Staffordshire University

At Staffordshire University we believe that a strong relationship between businesses and universities is essential in enabling the UK to maintain its competitiveness. Established in 1992, spanning two campuses in the heart of the West Midlands region, we have evolved into one of the country's most dynamic, progressive and forward-thinking learning institutions.

Our vision is to ensure that we are a crucial part of regional and urban economic regeneration and play a fundamental role in helping businesses to thrive, grow and survive economic downturn.

Through initiatives such as the "futures programme", delivered in collaboration with local business networks, we have supported the business and workforce community through short courses and knowledge network activity. Our pioneering work to support young graduate start-up business in the region so far has resulted in the creation of 163 new businesses in the last three years and the University continues to encourage entrepreneurship with cross-campus business incubation units and business support programmes.

We understand the importance of nurturing innovation and through our virtual knowledge hub, businesses can benefit from fresh thinking, ground-breaking research and world-class expertise within all aspects of their business. Applied Research Centres help companies innovate and compete in key technology areas such as digital media, design, mobile computing, electronics, security and medical technologies. The recently conceived "mobile fusion" project includes the development of a theatre management demonstrator system. This system aims to enhance the hospital patient journey in and out of theatre with a set of tools that improve communication between medical staff and perfect theatre utilisation, which reduces waste and could potentially decrease patient waiting lists.

Award-winning Knowledge Transfer Partnerships (KTPs) in innovation have transformed businesses, facilitating access to the knowledge and skills of academic staff, through high calibre associates. Since their inception, Staffordshire University has facilitated over 60 KTPs. We continue to manage new and existing projects for local and regional businesses working in partnership with the University. A project with West Midlands based company Scientific and Chemical Supplies Ltd, involved the development of forensic kits for schools, challenging the idea that "science is boring" by introducing students to the tools that are used for forensic activity, placing themselves at the forefront of the market for science teaching materials.

In addition to helping businesses to improve their competitive edge, the University values partnerships that assist businesses to improve their environmental impact. We work with the Renewable Energy Supply Chain Opportunities (RESCO) programme that provides regional businesses with the support they need to enter or expand into the supply chain markets of low carbon and renewable energy technologies.

01782 294178
forbusiness@staffs.ac.uk

Case study

The development of forensic kits for schools

Bilston-based company Scientific and Chemical Supplies Ltd (SciChem) supplies science education equipment and resources in the UK. They provide a wide range of laboratory equipment, chemicals and science education products uniquely to the primary, secondary and tertiary education and laboratory sectors. SciChem identified the opportunity to differentiate themselves from their competitors by supplying individually tailored solutions in products and services.

Through a Knowledge Transfer Partnership with the Faculty of Sciences at Staffordshire University and a postgraduate KTP associate, a specialist forensic kit for schools was developed. By using real life situations and crime scene scenarios the kit enables pupils to take on the role of the forensic scientist. It contains all the necessary components to make science "fun" and facilitates the opportunity for training in the use of these products and in the underlying scientific theories. Student and teacher versions of the instructional information make it a great resource for busy teaching and technical staff.

SciChem developed a new product development (NPD) department with the scientific and educational competence to design products prepared for individual course curricula. The products and educational materials show the relevance to real life situations and demonstrate that studying science can enhance employability potential.

SciChem has grown to be the market leader for the supply of these teaching materials to the secondary school market. The KTP also enabled them to go beyond just the supplying of resources, to become a company that can also bring new products to the market. The company have moved to a position where they are starting to drive the direction of new science and teaching products in response to curriculum opportunities. The implementation of smarter working practices has led to improved flexibility and productivity and after the first year SciChem sold in excess of 1,100 forensic kits.

The partnership has taken them in a fresh direction and enabled them to create a new position within the company of product development manager, which the KTP associate was appointed to. It has shown that through research and collaboration with a university, companies can tap into the broader product market and successfully differentiate themselves from the competition.

Tim Avery, education sales director at SciChem said: "It started a process of moving us from a supplier to a developer and manufacturer of exclusive materials, and has enabled us to establish our new product development department. Our relationship with Staffordshire University now provides us with the platform for future development."

The success of the Knowledge Transfer Partnership with SciChem led to an award for "innovation achieved" at the 2010 Lord Stafford Awards.

Profile

Dragon Innovation Partnership Profile

The Dragon Innovation Partnership is a collaboration between Swansea Metropolitan University, Swansea University and University of Wales Trinity Saint David. It aims to help businesses access relevant expertise across the partner institutions to discuss their development, support and training needs. The organisations involved then receive tailor-made support packages to help them achieve their aims.

The key benefit from this bespoke service is that from whatever point an organisation accesses the partnership, they will be directed to the person with the right skills to meet their needs. The partnership's key role of identifying opportunities for transferring knowledge and expertise between experts and organisations is enhanced by the individual expertise and strengths of the three partner institutions.

Swansea Metropolitan University has exceptional skills in applied design and engineering, as well as art and design, and also has a strong commercial training background.

Swansea University has a celebrated history of successful knowledge transfer projects, and is a leader in the fields of engineering, computer science, medicine and health science, environmental technologies and sustainability, and business and law.

University of Wales Trinity Saint David is a highly respected provider of quality bilingual training and development for SMEs and communities. With strengths in education, tourism, creative and cultural industries, and work-based learning, Wales' newest (and oldest!) university boosts the wealth of intelligence on offer.

The broad range of skills and expertise on offer at the three universities makes the Dragon Innovation Partnership the perfect place for both business and community organisations to start when looking for help to solve strategic business problems. The partnership has established a good track record for supporting businesses, organisations and academics alike; organising and hosting a range of successful seminars, workshops and events to promote available funding streams – and transferring knowledge from those who have expertise, to those that need expertise.

When asked what had been the most successful or positive aspects of their involvement with the Dragon Innovation Partnership, businesses highlighted the attitude of staff and provision of information, which had led to links being established with one university or several universities. Comments included: "Listening, understanding, flexible delivery"; "Good communications"; "Responsiveness to our concerns and questions. Ability to acknowledge the gain on both sides of academia/industry collaborations. Approachable representatives who provide clear answers and direction"; "Understood the potential need of businesses and where universities could assist and vice versa."

Commercial services, Swansea Metropolitan University; commercialservices@smu.ac.uk or 01792 481163.
Department of Research and Innovation, Swansea University; researchandinnovation@swansea.ac.uk or 01792 606060.
Research and Development Office, University of Wales, Trinity Saint David; researchanddevelopment@tsd.ac.uk or 01267 676867.

Dragon Innovation Partnership
www.dragonip.ac.uk

Case study

Dr Steve Conlan, Director of the NanoHealth Centre at Swansea University, met north Wales based company Porvair at a networking event arranged by the Dragon Innovation Partnership and identified that one of their products had considerable potential for the life science sector.

Description and purpose

Dr Conlan had discussions with one of the Dragon Innovation Partnership's knowledge transfer officers to identify the most appropriate knowledge transfer route. A KTP was the most appropriate mechanism for their company because of its focus on business benefits. A funding bid was prepared jointly by Dr Conlan, a representative of Porvair and the Partnership's knowledge transfer officer. Porvair made it clear that they wanted to achieve excellence which the Dragon Innovation Partnership was able to provide.

Dr Conlan and Porvair subsequently developed a greater understanding of each other's needs and aims and, together with IG Innovations and Abertawe Bro Morgannwg University NHS Trust in the form of Singleton Hospital, have successfully won a collaborative industrial research project (CIRP) from the Welsh government.

Results and outcomes

Swansea University Centre for NanoHealth and Porvair were awarded a KTP, which was funded by BBSRC (Biotechnology and Biological Sciences Research Council) and the Welsh government. This collaboration will, "bring Porvair up to speed with epigenetics and develop a novel project which brings together life-science and engineering technologies", says Dr Conlan.

The CIRP gave Porvair access to antibodies that are specific to the products being developed by the KTP. It will also benefit the other partners: IG Innovations will gain access to an innovation pipeline for the antibodies it produces; Singleton Hospital will be able to test and use the technologies and Swansea University will benefit from new research.

The Dragon Innovation Partnership was instrumental in identifying and obtaining the CIRP funding.

The Centre for NanoHealth and the Dragon Innovation Partnership collaborated in other ways, including presenting funding opportunities at the centre's events.

The Partnership knew that the centre had the capacity and infrastructure to work with businesses, which will lead to more opportunities being realised in the future. The Dragon Innovation Partnership adds real value to collaboration, by understanding the needs of both business and academia.

Profile

Teesside University

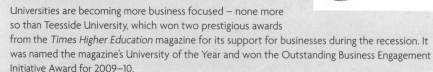

Universities are becoming more business focused – none more so than Teesside University, which won two prestigious awards from the *Times Higher Education* magazine for its support for businesses during the recession. It was named the magazine's University of the Year and won the Outstanding Business Engagement Initiative Award for 2009–10.

Now, it is expanding its work to build on the early signs of business recovery in the north-east with developments such as the re-opening of Redcar blast furnace by inward investor SSI and the planned arrival of Hitachi in County Durham, in 2014.

But, as Laura Woods, director of the University's Department of Academic Enterprise, acknowledges: "Growing business in this economic climate is still going to be a challenge. We recognise at Teesside that, more than ever, universities need to work with business to grow a high-skill, high-value economy.

"At the height of the banking crisis in 2009, we came up with a 16-point plan to help businesses. Working with partners such as further education colleges, we made it our business to respond flexibly and quickly to innovation and training needs to help deliver bottom-line benefits. It's an approach we've continued because it works."

Companies are helped to introduce innovative technologies, and improve workforce skills in areas such as leadership and management.

More intensive support has come through Knowledge Transfer Partnerships, which are two to three-year problem-solving projects that see a company, graduate and academic expert working together to increase competitiveness. Often, a graduate internship is just what employers need to plug a skills deficit or resources gap. Last year, 250 graduates were placed with organisations, and thanks to the European Regional Development Fund, a new scheme will help over 400 SMEs in the north-east over the next three years.

Laura Woods says: "Companies benefit from graduate expertise. Interns come out with hugely enhanced work-based skills – and in most cases it leads to a permanent job: a win-win result."

Companies working with Teesside University include Northumbrian Water, which is collaboratively developing innovative solutions to re-use and recycle water treatment sludge.

Another is Washington-based Griffith Textile Machines. Technical director Chris Clarke says: "Our relationship with the University began when we had difficulty finding a fresh graduate for a new opening. It was Teesside which gave us the best response."

In the last year, the University has also helped its graduates and staff create 90 new companies, with start-up levels expected to grow as entrepreneurs@tees, a new initiative with the Students' Union, encourages more students to become entrepreneurs.

"It's all about using our strengths to add real value to business," says Laura.

01642 384068
business@tees.ac.uk
www.tees.ac.uk/spark

Case study

A Teesside University partnership with business has been hailed as one of the best in the country. The Knowledge Transfer Partnership (KTP) with engineering company Stanley Vickers Ltd was judged as "outstanding" by the Technology Strategy Board. Fewer than 5% of KTPs get the top grade nationwide.

It also led to graduate Sara Zarei joining the Middlesbrough-based firm as its operations and improvements engineer, after increasing the company's efficiency and production potential.

Teesside graduate Sara Zarei, left, with Professor Farhad Nabhani, centre, and David Ford, Production Manager at Stanley Vickers Ltd

Sara, who holds a prestigious "business leader of tomorrow" award, is also completing a PhD on the application of automatic identification and data capture systems.

She originally joined the company as a KTP associate after graduating with distinction from Teesside University's MSc Computer-aided Engineering.

Stanley Vickers specialises in manufacturing and refurbishing precision screws and barrels for the plastic, rubber and food industries. The 60-year-old company turned to the University after struggling to keep up with demand for its products.

Sara believes the recession helped the KTP. "It changed people's mindset. They realised that if we didn't change some of our old ways the company might not survive."

Production manager David Ford says: "We're delighted the KTP has been awarded the top grade. It encouraged us to adopt a more modern approach to introducing new technology and opened our minds to new ways of working.

"We've seen vast improvements in the company's processes and machinery through the KTP project and it has led to large financial savings. As well as offering Sara a permanent post, we've taken on four new apprentices and are looking for another graduate.

"Since the KTP finished last year, production is up by 50% and I only wish we could start another one with the University."

David jointly managed the project with Farhad Nabhani, Professor of biomechanics and manufacturing, who says: "We're delighted with the 'outstanding' award. The project was particularly successful for all three stakeholders. As well as direct company benefits, it has given the University excellent learning and teaching material and established Sara on a wonderful career path."

Debbie Buckley-Golder, head of knowledge exchange at the Technology Strategy Board, says: "The 'outstanding' grade is a mark of real quality for Knowledge Transfer Partnerships. It's clear to see that this project with Stanley Vickers has delivered substantial benefits for all partners and this accolade is amply deserved. Congratulations to the whole team on a fantastic collaboration."

Profile

University of Ulster

The University of Ulster is a modern and progressive institution and is currently pre-eminent across the island of Ireland in knowledge transfer and new venture formation.

With campuses in Northern Ireland, Coleraine, Jordanstown, Derry and Belfast, the University of Ulster is deeply embedded in every aspect of life and work in Northern Ireland.

Ulster has six faculties: Arts; Art, Design and the Built Environment; Ulster Business School; Computing and Engineering; Life and Health Sciences; and Social Sciences, and over 25,000 students.

Engaging with industry

The university provides a focus for enterprise innovation, networking, research, training and development projects, consultancy and funded programmes.

Business liaison managers work in partnership with clients to identify the right contacts within the University to help deliver innovative solutions to meet business needs.

We work with companies throughout the world to help them to capitalise on business opportunities and to prepare for global challenges. Our business and research partner portfolio includes companies such as Boeing, Bombardier Aerospace, BT, GSK, Microsoft, Rolls-Royce, and SAP.

Ulster's track record in consultancy is grounded in its excellent reputation in the arts, science, engineering, social sciences and business sectors. This reputation extends to Ulster's ability to mobilise multidisciplinary teams to assist clients. Our innovative consultancy policy allows academics to commit a generous proportion of their time to business assignments. This ensures connectivity with the business community, that real world issues are included on the teaching portfolio and that research is aligned with future business needs.

We work with business providing access to expertise, research excellence and state-of-the-art facilities as well as delivering high quality graduates. Our goal is to help businesses achieve their potential.

Research collaboration

The University is a significant provider of outsourced research and development to businesses in Northern Ireland and overseas. Ulster's research capacity continues to increase in terms of its quality and strength.

Ulster's four campuses are home to 16 Research Institutes specialising in areas such as health and rehabilitation sciences, intelligent systems, coastal and marine research and art and design. These institutes have been established to harness high quality research expertise to ensure the research capability of the University performs at the highest possible level.

We have a network of strategic partnerships throughout the world. Technology and knowledge transfer and commercial exploitation of ideas are promoted by the Office of Innovation through a range of initiatives and ongoing research and consultancy with business and industry.

Office of Innovation
028 9036 8019
enquiry@ulster.ac.uk
http://oi.ulster.ac.uk/

Case study

Collaborative research: BMSRI and Randox Laboratories Ltd

Randox Laboratories is an international clinical diagnostics company that provides innovative solutions to laboratories worldwide. Randox's diagnostics division is specifically focused on developing high quality diagnostic products that provide for increased efficiency, accuracy and reliability. In particular, Randox's biochip array technology has been at the forefront of multiplex array development, combining award-winning analysers with low density, highly characterised panels of DNA, RNA or protein biomarkers providing diagnostic, predictive or prognostic information to the healthcare provider.

In recent years, Ulster's Biomedical Sciences Research Institute (BMSRI) has developed a strong relationship with Randox resulting in a number of collaborative research projects with the company's diagnostics division.

One of these is biomarkers for rheumatoid arthritis (RA). Ulster presented compelling evidence to Randox in relation to its biomarker discoveries for RA. This, combined with the current approach of using trial and error for RA therapy, convinced Randox that the development of an array that can stratify patient response to anti-TNF therapy (a treatment for severe RA patients), represented an excellent business opportunity for the company.

As a result, the parties have entered into a two-year collaborative R&D project, which has successfully secured funding of more than £1m from the Technology Strategy Board. This innovative theranostic RA array will provide Randox with a powerful introduction into the inflammatory medicine sector, in which there is an urgent clinical need to better manage RA patients, through more tailored therapy. Part of the project will be undertaken at the Clinical Translational Research and Innovation Centre (C-TRIC) at Altnagelvin Hospital. The centre, which has been established through a unique partnership between the University of Ulster, Derry City Council and the Western Health and Social Care Trust, aims to promote and facilitate translational and clinical research, the primary objective of which is to reduce both the time to market and the costs associated with research and development of innovative health technologies, medical devices and therapeutics. C-TRIC is particularly well placed to support this R&D as it facilitates access to high quality clinical materials and data required for personalised medicine.

The overall aim of these collaborative research projects is to translate the unique research at Ulster into clinically useful personalised medicine tools for incorporation in existing or newly developed Randox platforms.

Profile

University of Westminster

How can the University of Westminster help your company realise its creative ideas, and track down the leading edge knowledge that will contribute to your business?

We have three main ways to help. We can:

- up the value of your people while enhancing their careers
- source young talent to work with you short term
- design ground-breaking schemes to radically improve your company's future.

Why lose valuable and talented members of staff, for lack of one important skill? Why not nurture your staff by helping them fulfil their potential? The University of Westminster has a variety of courses available, to enable companies to plug any skill gaps. From basic training to postgraduate study, we can help you brush up the talents in your workforce.

What about quick projects? We have aspiring young undergraduates and postgraduates who are interested in placements or internships. Think what they could do for your company. Give our dedicated careers service the spec, and we will come up with the best available talent.

How about something more fundamental? Radical rethinks in companies are often restricted by resources. But in these days of huge technological advances, there is massive scope for improving efficiency, effectiveness and profitability. So don't let the opportunity pass you by. Our KTP Unit can help your business fly by creating profit for you – at a very favourable price.

A KTP is a contract between one of our departments and you, which engages a highly qualified recent graduate on a project of strategic importance to your business. By harnessing our top academics, the KTP will connect you to the latest expertise and cutting-edge business thinking.

What's more the government contributes significantly to these partnerships. They pay 66% upfront and they also can give you significant tax credits to soften the impact of your contribution.

The KTP might:

- focus on the development of your products or services
- enhance the skills of your staff, thus boosting in-house knowledge
- use emerging internet technologies to catapult your company into the top league
- design path finding schemes that could be scaled up to cover your whole enterprise.

For over 20 years the KTP unit has been applying their knowledge in real-world settings. They have fostered mutual opportunities between various companies, industry and the University of Westminster. And their established track record has provided strong networks to champion leading edge innovation.

Beyond the individual partnerships, the KTP unit keeps abreast of the many high impact projects springing up countrywide. It is linked into several of the national Knowledge Transfer Networks set up by the Technology Strategy Board to share information online.

The future of the UK lies in such constructive links between academia and business.

KTP Unit
028 7911 5865
d.c.carroll@westminster.ac.uk

Case study

Rawlinson Kelly Whittlestone (now part of EC Harris)

In 2004 Rawlinson Kelly Whittlestone Ltd was a small consultancy well known for providing a wide range of healthcare planning advice for the NHS and the private sector. But they realised that in order to get ahead of the competition they needed further skills in both data analysis and simulation modelling.

Their plan was to develop tools for a variety of healthcare processes so that they could advise both public and private sector clients on the best mix of space, staff and resources to be both efficient and effective.

Westminster's School of Computer Science came to their aid with a Knowledge Transfer Partnership (KTP) to produce a flexible model that covered all aspects of planning, be it single departments or whole hospitals.

For example, planning an effective A+E department requires statistics on the health of the surrounding population to establish the nature of demand. For the best practical layout RKW can model variations in opening hours, staffing levels, types of equipment used, the most convenient location for that equipment ... and more.

The project has been a roaring success. It has given RKW technological skills that match their understanding of healthcare. They can accurately gauge the size of the hospital for the catchment area, produce an efficient layout for the building, and illustrate their designs in action with dynamic graphical reporting techniques.

The software is invaluable for RKW's clients, private sector bidders who want to present their proposals, healthcare providers who want to improve their operational efficiency and it is also a great marketing tool for RKW.

RKW's business plan had always been to look for a strategic alliance with another company. When they started discussions with EC Harris towards the end of the KTP, the new simulation modelling techniques were undoubtedly a jewel in their crown!

Reynolds Porter Chamberlain

Reynolds Porter Chamberlain LLP (RPC) is a large firm of City lawyers, with special expertise in the areas of insurance, reinsurance, commercial and corporate legal services. The advice they give clients, here and abroad, involves understanding the specific context of the individual client.

It is a truism that developing a brand means establishing a reputation that's consistent for all their people. To do this they know that the more they can share any rare insights with their colleagues, the more collectively expert RPC will be.

That is why RPC have welcomed a KTP with the University of Westminster to develop their use of social media tools and techniques. At far less than the normal cost of such a project, Westminster's Business School is working with RPC to design a social-based intranet that, like a twitter stream, will show people what is going on within the firm, without deluging everyone with emails. Most importantly, it is enabling partners to take insights gained individually and make use of them collectively for the benefit of their clients.

The initiative is putting RPC ahead of the game. At the Knowledge Management UK 2011 Awards, RPC's new cutting-edge intranet won them the award for the Best Knowledge Management Initiative or Implementation in a Professional Services Firm.

PART 7
Appendices

Appendix 1

University spin-out IPOs (initial public offerings) and trade sales, 2003–11

Courtesy of *The Review*, PraxisUnico

	Company	University	Market	IPO Value	Money raised	Date
2003	Wolfson Micro	Edinburgh	LSE	£214m	£25.3m	Oct
			[TH]Total	[TH]£214m	[TH]£25.3m	
2004	ARK Therapeutics	UCL	LSE	£168m	£55m	Mar
	OHM	Southampton	AIM	£49m	£10m	Mar
	Vectura	Bath	AIM	£60m	£20m	Jun
	Summit	Oxford	AIM	£42m	£15m	Oct
	Synairgen	Southampton	AIM	£28m	£10.5m	Oct
	Ceres Power	Imperial	AIM	£66m	£21.6m	Nov
	IDMos	Dundee/St Andrews	AIM	£20m	£5m	Nov
	Microemissive Displays	Edinburgh/ Napier	AIM	£25.7m	£15.7m	
	Andor	Queen's Belfast	AIM	£23m	£4.5m	Dec
	Cambridge Display Technology	Cambridge	NASDAQ	$234m (£122m)	£15.6m	Dec
			Total	**£603.7m**	**£172.9m**	

	Company	University	Market	IPO Value	Money raised	Date
2005	FusionIP	Sheffield	AIM	£28m	£8.2m	Jan
	Proximagen	KCL	AIM	£29.7m	£14.5m	Mar
	Provexis	Rowett Research Institute	AIM[1]	£14m	£5.9m[2]	Jun
	Stem Cell Sciences	Edinburgh	AIM	£21.2m	£6.0m	Jul
	Oxonica	Oxford	AIM	£35.3m	£7.1m	Jul
	ReNeuron	KCL	AIM	£23.4m	£9.5m	Aug
	NeuroDiscovery	Warwick	Australian	£3.1m[3]	£0.63m	Aug
	GETECH	Leeds	AIM	£10.8m	£3.5m	Sep
	SPI Lasers	Southampton	AIM	£25.5m	£12m	Oct
	Celoxica	Oxford	AIM	£16.1m	£6.1m	Oct
	Toumaz[4]	Imperial College	AIM	£17.7m	£7.1m	Nov
			Total	**£224.8m**	**£80.5m**	
2006	Lipoxen	School of Pharmacy, London	AIM	£13.2m	£3.78m	Jan
	Syntopix	Leeds	AIM	£10.1m	£4.0m	Mar
	ParOS	Imperial	AIM	£16.5m	-	Mar
	Renovo	Manchester	LSE	£154m	£50m	Apr
	Oxford Catalysts	Oxford	AIM	£65m	£15m	Apr
	Avacta	Leeds	AIM[5]	£15m	£1.013m	Jul
	Imperial Innovations	Imperial	AIM	£180.8m	£25m	Jul
	ValiRx	Imperial	AIM	£12.8	-	Oct
			Total	**£467.4m**	**£98.8m**	
2007	Epistem	Manchester	AIM	£8.1m	£3m	Apr
	Modern Water	Surrey/Cardiff	AIM	£70m	£30m	Jun
	Tracsis	Leeds	AIM	£7m	£2m	Nov
	e-Therapeutics	Newcastle	AIM	£37.3m	£1.3m	Nov

	Company	University	Market	IPO Value	Money raised	Date
	Oxford Advanced Surfaces Group	Oxford	AIM	£44.5m	£3m	Dec
			Total	£166.9m	£39.3m	
2008	Scancell	Nottingham	PLUS[6]	£6.1m	£1.6m	Sep
			Total	£6.1m	£1.6m	
2009	Nanoco Group	Manchester	AIM	£38.6m	£8.1m	Apr
			Total	£38.6m	£8.1m	
2010	Ilika	Southampton	AIM	£18.7m	£5.2m	Apr
	Tissue Regenix[7]	Sheffield	AIM	£23.3m	£4.5m	Jun
			Total	£42.0m	£9.7m	
2011	Microsaic Systems	Imperial	AIM	£12m	£4.0m	Apr
			Total	£12m	£4.0m	
Grand Total				£1775.5m	£440.2m	

Notes

1. Reverse merger with Nutrinnovator plc.
2. £3.8m raised plus £2.1m loan for equity swap.
3. At A$1 = 42.5p.
4. Reverse merger with Nanoscience plc.
5. Reverse takeover of Readybuy plc.
6. Transferred to AIM on 30 July 2010.
7. Reverse takeover of Oxeco.

Trade sales

Acquisitions	University	Acquirer	Price	Date
Kudos Pharma	Cambridge/CRT	Astra Zeneca	£121m	December 2005
NeuTech	Manchester	Novartis	£305.1m	June 2006
Cambridge Antibody Technology	MRC	Astra Zeneca	£702m[8]	August 2006
Domantis	MRC	GSK	£230m	December 2006
Solexa	Cambridge	Illumina	£306m ($600m)	January 2007
Arrow Therapeutics	UCL/Newcastle	Astra Zeneca	£76m ($150m)	February 2007
Daniolabs	Cambridge	VASTox	£15m	March 2007
Plasso Technology	Sheffield	BD	Not disclosed	May 2007
MTEM	Edinburgh	Petroleum Geo-Services	£138m ($275m)	June 2007
Cambridge Display Technology	Cambridge	Sumitomo	£140m ($285m)	July 2007
Meridio	Queens Belfast	Autonomy	£20m	November 2007
CamFPD	Cambridge	Microsoft	£10m	November 2007
OMD	Oxford	Avacta	£3m	November 2007
SIW	UCL	MDY Healthcare	£12.5m	February 2008
Transitive	Manchester	IBM	Not disclosed	December 2008
Thiakis	Imperial	Wyeth (Pfizer)	£99.6m	December 2008
Phototherapeutics	Manchester	Photomedex Inc	£14m ($20m)	February 2009
Biotec Laboratories	Nottingham	Lab21	Not disclosed	March 2009
APT	Queens Belfast	Audemat	Not disclosed	March 2009
Inforsense	Imperial	IDBS	£5m	June 2009

Acquisitions	University	Acquirer	Price	Date
BioAnaLab	Oxford	Millipore	Not disclosed	July 2009
Orthomemetics	Cambridge/MIT	TiGenix	£14.9m (€16.3m)	December 2009
Reactivelab	Glasgow	Avacta	£5m	March 2010
Apatech	QMU	Baxter	£220m ($330m)	March 2010
MET	Imperial	Evonik Industries AG	£4.5m	March 2010
Im-Sense	UEA	Not disclosed (rumoured to be Apple)	Not disclosed	July 2010
Exosect (Bee Health Division)	Southampton	Bayer Cropscience	Not disclosed	November 2010
Artemis Intelligent Power	Edinburgh	Mitsubishi Heavy Industries	Not disclosed[9]	December 2010
Biovex	UCL	Amgen	£632m ($1Bn[10])	January 2011
Lab901	Edinburgh	Agilent	Not disclosed	February 2011
Chameleon Biosurfaces	PBL/John Innes	Not disclosed	Not disclosed	March 2011
Grand Total			**>£3074m**	
Pending Acquisitions				
Astex Therapeutics	Cambridge	SuperGen	£33.7m[11] ($55m+)	July 2011 close

Notes

8. Astra Zeneca already owned 19.2% of CAT and paid £567m to acquire the remaining 80.8% of the company.
9. Included commitment to invest £100m over 5 years.
10. $425m cash and $575m future payments.
11. Announced 6 April 2011 with expected closure July 2011. $25m cash, $30m future payments and 35% of post acquisition stock of Supergen.

Appendix 2

Model agreements for university–business research collaboration

Courtesy of the Intellectual Property Office

Templates and models for intellectual property

The Intellectual Property Office offers several templates and model agreements to assist industry/university collaboration.

The Lambert Toolkit, built on the collective experience of the UK's technology transfer community, offers a set of model agreements. They each provide a different approach in key areas of who owns, and has the right to exploit, the intellectual property in the results of the collaborative project. There are five Model Research Collaboration Agreements (One to One) and a Decision Guide to help choose the right agreement. Most commonly used is Lambert Agreement 1 (university owns the IP and gives industry a non-exclusive licence to use it). Lambert Agreement 4 represents the opposite relationship and is usually used where the industry party provides the major funding resource to the project. Lambert Agreement 5 covers contract research where industry owns the IP and the university retains no rights to publish research without the sponsor's permission. In Lambert Agreements 2 and 3 the university owns the IP for which industry can negotiate an exclusive licence or an assignment to exploit.

None of the five Research Collaboration Agreements deals with joint ownership of IP because this occurs more rarely than people think and is more difficult for both industry and the university to manage. However, of the four Lambert Model Consortium Agreements (Multi-Party), Consortium Agreement A contains an example of a joint ownership provision. It is important that the Agreement sets out what rights each joint owner has to exploit the IP. The four Lambert Model Consortium Agreements reflect the same structure as the five Research Agreements, but contain additional provisions to cover some of the complications that arise as a result of having more than two parties.

The IPO also offers template examples of other agreements such as:

- a Patent Assignment (for example, where industry and the university reach agreement under Lambert Agreement 3 that the university will assign IP in certain results of research collaboration to industry)

- a Consultancy Agreement (for example, when an individual researcher undertakes to provide consultancy services to a commercial sponsor).

The five Lambert Model Agreements for research collaboration

LMA	Terms	IP owner
1	Business has non-exclusive rights to use in specified field of technology and/or geographical territory; no sub-licences	University
2	Business may negotiate further licence to some or all University IP	University
3	Business may negotiate for an assignment of some University IP	University
4	University has right to use for non-commercial purposes	Business
5	Contract research: no publication by University without business's permission	Business

The Lambert Model Consortium Agreements

Lambert Model Consortium Agreement	Terms
Agreement A	Each member of the Consortium owns the IP in the Results that it creates and grants each of the other parties a non-exclusive licence to use those Results for the purposes of the Project and for any other purpose.
Agreement B	The other parties assign their IP in the Results to the lead Exploitation Party who undertakes to exploit the Results. (Alternatively the Lead Exploitation Party is granted an exclusive licence.)
Agreement C	Each party takes an assignment of IP in the Results that are germane to its core business and undertakes to exploit those Results.
Agreement D	Each member of the Consortium owns the IP in the Results that it creates and grants each of the other parties a non-exclusive licence to use those Results for the purposes of the Project only. If any member of the Consortium wishes to negotiate a licence to allow it to exploit the IP of another member or to take an assignment of that IP, the owner of that IP undertakes to negotiate a licence or assignment.

Other useful resources for business–university collaborations

	Resource	Example of when used
1	Sample Patent and Know-how Licence	Where the Sponsor and the University have reached agreement that the Sponsor should be granted an exclusive licence to use identified IP in the results of a research collaboration (see Lambert Model Agreement 2).
2	Sample Patent Assignment	Where the Sponsor and the University have reached agreement that the University will assign IP in certain Results of a research collaboration to the Sponsor (see Lambert Model Agreement 3). It is based on the assumption that the Assignee will pay a one-off sum for the assignment of the Patent, but the parties may agree revenue sharing or other payment terms.
3	Sample Materials Transfer Agreement	Where a Sponsor has agreed to allow the University to use certain materials in connection with a research project.

	Resource	Example of when used
4	Sample Consultancy Agreement	Where there is an agreement between a commercial Sponsor and an individual academic researcher, under which the individual researcher undertakes to provide consultancy services to the Sponsor. It records a private arrangement between the researcher and the Sponsor. The researcher assigns the intellectual property rights in the work he does as a consultant to the Sponsor in return for payments made by the Sponsor. In order to be able to assign those rights, the researcher must own them. That normally means that they must not have been developed in the course of his or her employment by the university; if they have been developed in the course of his employment, those rights will usually belong to the university.
5	Sample Non-Disclosure Agreement	Where a Business and a University wish to exchange confidential information as part of their discussions about a potential research project before they have entered into a Collaboration Agreement.
6	Sample Equipment Loan Agreement	Where the Business Sponsor has agreed to allow the University to use equipment in connection with a research project.
7	Sample Confidentiality Notice	A simple example of the kind of notification a user would include on the front page of a document to indicate that it and the information provided are confidential.

Further details: www.ipo.gov.uk/lambert

Appendix 3
The support network

The **Technology Strategy Board** is the UK's national innovation agency. Its goal is to accelerate economic growth by stimulating and supporting business-led innovation. It works right across government, business and the research community – removing barriers to innovation, bringing organisations together to focus on opportunities, running competitions for research, and investing in the development of new technology-based products and services for future markets. Further details: www.innovateuk.org.

Knowledge Transfer Partnerships (KTP) is Europe's leading programme in helping businesses to improve their competitiveness, productivity and performance through collaboration and knowledge transfer between business and academia. Run through the universities under the auspices of the Technology Strategy Board, its funding goes toward identifying innovative solutions that can help businesses to grow. Further details: www.innovateuk.org/deliveringinnovation/ knowledgetransferpartnerships.ashx.

Knowledge Transfer Networks (KTNs) are designed to engineer a meeting of minds between business and research. Within a national framework co-ordinated by the Technology Strategy Board, 15 specialist groups bring together the right people with the right knowledge at the right time. Further details: www.innovateuk.org/ deliveringinnovation/knowledgetransfernetworks.ashx.

The **Intellectual Property Office (IPO)** is the official government body responsible for intellectual property (IP) rights in the United Kingdom. These rights include trademarks, patents, designs and copyright. The IPO offers a range of products and services to support businesses; these include an IP Healthcheck diagnostic tool, a range of free booklets, newsletters, workshops and seminars. Further details: www.ipo.gov.uk or 0300 300 2000.

Research Councils UK (RCUK) is the strategic partnership of the UK's seven Research Councils who annually invest around £3bn in research. They support excellent research, as judged by peer review, which has an impact on the growth, prosperity and well-being of the UK. To maintain the UK's global research position they offer a diverse range of funding opportunities, foster international collaborations and provide access to the best facilities and infrastructure around the world. They also support the training and career development of researchers and work with them to inspire young people and engage the wider public with research. To maximise the impact of research on economic growth and societal well-being, they work in partnership with other research funders including the Technology Strategy Board, the UK Higher Education Funding Councils, business, government, and charitable organisations. For further details, visit www.rcuk.ac.uk.

The seven UK Research Councils are:

- Arts & Humanities Research Council (AHRC)
- Biotechnology & Biological Sciences Research Council (BBSRC)
- Economic & Social Research Council (ESRC)
- Engineering & Physical Sciences Research Council (EPSRC)
- Medical Research Council (MRC)
- Natural Environment Research Council (NERC)
- Science & Technology Facilities Council (STFC)

Universities UK is the representative body for the executive heads of UK universities and is recognised as the umbrella group for the university sector. It works to advance the interests of universities and to spread good practice throughout the higher education sector. Universities UK is a company limited by guarantee with charitable status. UUK members are the executive heads (vice-chancellors or principals) of UK universities and colleges of higher education. UUK currently has 133 members. Further details: www.universitiesuk.ac.uk.

PraxisUnico is the UK's leading association for research commercialisation professionals, working as an educational not-for-profit organisation set up to support innovation and commercialisation of public sector and charity research for social and economic impact. PraxisUnico encourages innovation and acts as a voice for the research commercialisation profession, facilitating the interaction between the public sector research base, business and government. PraxisUnico provides a forum for best practice exchange, underpinned by first-class training and development programmes. Further details: www.praxisunico.org.uk.

Interface – the knowledge connection for business – is a matchmaking service connecting businesses quickly and easily to world-class expertise, knowledge and research facilities available in Scotland's universities and research institutes. Interface's free and impartial service stimulates innovation and encourages companies to consider academic support to help solve their business challenges. Open to all, regardless of sector or geographical location, Interface proves that collaborating with academic partners brings significant business benefits including increased competitiveness, the introduction of a new product or service and company expansion. If you have a specific business challenge – technical, process or strategic – Interface will help you access the knowledge and facilities available from Scotland's universities and research institutes. To find out more and view our client case studies, visit www.interface-online.org.uk or email info@interface-online.org.uk.

The **British Library Business & IP Centre** in London launched in March 2006 and supports entrepreneurs, inventors and small businesses from that first spark of inspiration to successfully launching and developing a business. Since the launch, over 250,000 entrepreneurs have used the Centre. Further details: www.bl.uk/bipc.

AURIL is the professional association representing all practitioners involved in knowledge creation, development and exchange in the UK and Ireland who work to ensure that new ideas, technologies and innovations flow from their institution into the marketplace. It is the largest knowledge transfer association in Europe, with more than 1,600 members from universities, NHS Trusts and public sector research establishments. The Association enjoys widespread international recognition through its success in influencing UK government policy. It has strong working relations with the Confederation of British Industry, Universities UK, the UKIPO, the Department for Business, Innovation and Skills (BIS), HM Treasury and Higher Education Funding Councils, in partnership with whom it has produced many publications. Further details: www.auril.org.uk.

The **Institute of Knowledge Transfer (IKT)** is the sector's body devoted to supporting and promoting the profession of knowledge transfer, fostering greater understanding of knowledge transfer and enhancing the status of those involved in the profession. It is dedicated solely to meeting the needs of the individuals involved in knowledge transfer; the professionals which make this dynamic new industry. The IKT will set standards for development of the profession and address issues surrounding accreditation, certification and training. Further details: www.ikt.org.uk.

The **Department for Business Innovations and Skills (BIS)** brings all of the levers of the economy together in one place and its policy areas can all help to drive growth. Among its aims are the following.

- It is committed to fostering world-class higher education to provide the nation with the high level skills needed for economic success, while ensuring excellence in teaching and research.

- It aims to create a high quality and responsive further education sector that equips workers with the skills demanded in a modern globalised economy.

- It pursues global excellence in science and research to help maintain economic prosperity and address key global and domestic challenges, such as climate change and security.

- It leads on the innovation agenda and is taking action to boost innovation in the economy and across the public sector, because it helps deal with complex challenges and drive growth by improving productivity and R&D.

Further details: www.bis.gov.uk.

The **Higher Education Funding Council for England (HEFCE)** distributes public money for research and teaching to universities and colleges in England that provide higher education. Established in 1992, it aims to promote high-quality education and research, within a financially healthy sector; it also plays a key role in ensuring accountability and promoting good practice.

HEFCE's work is informed by the three key principles of opportunity, choice and excellence, and its funds support three priorities in higher education: the core academic activities of learning and teaching, research and knowledge exchange. HEFCE aims to deliver these objectives through an emphasis on high-quality information, a proportionate approach to regulation, investment for public benefit, and a commitment to working in partnership with government, students, universities, colleges, and key national agencies – this includes working to develop the connections between higher education and the economy and society. Further details: www.hefce.ac.uk.

The **Scottish Further and Higher Education Funding Council (SFC)** is the national, strategic body that is responsible for funding teaching and learning provision, research and other activities in Scotland's 41 colleges and 19 universities and higher education institutions. Its mission is to invest in the development of a coherent college and university system which, through enhanced learning, research and knowledge exchange, leads to improved economic, educational, social, civic and cultural outcomes for the people of Scotland. Further details: www.sfc.ac.uk.

The **Higher Education Funding Council for Wales** is the Welsh government's agency for distributing funding for higher education in Wales. Its objectives are to develop and sustain internationally excellent higher education in Wales, for the benefit of individuals, society and the economy, in Wales and more widely. Resources are deployed to secure higher education (HE) learning and research of the highest quality, make the most of the contribution of HE to Wales's culture, society and economy and ensure high quality, accredited teacher training. Further details: www.hefcw.ac.uk.

Northern Ireland's **Department for Employment and Learning** promotes economic, social and personal development through high quality learning, research and skills training. Its four priorities are the following.

- Enhancing the provision of learning and skills, including entrepreneurship, enterprise, management and leadership.

- Increasing the level of research and development, creativity and innovation in the Northern Ireland economy.

- Helping individuals to acquire jobs, including self-employment, and improving the linkages between employment programmes and skills development.

- The development and maintenance of the framework of employment rights and responsibilities.

Further details: www.delni.gov.uk.

NESTA is the National Endowment for Science, Technology and the Arts, an independent body with a mission to make the UK more innovative. It invests in early-stage companies, informs policy, and delivers practical programmes that inspire others to solve the big challenges of the future. Further details: www.nesta.org.uk.

National Council for Graduate Entrepreneurship (NCGE) is focused on graduates starting businesses, and on understanding, developing and promoting a culture of entrepreneurship within higher education through research, education and facilitation. Further details: www.ncee.org.uk.

The **National Consortium of University Entrepreneurs (NACUE)** is a national organisation that supports and represents university enterprise societies and student entrepreneurs to drive the growth of entrepreneurship across the UK. Further details: www.nacue.com.

Appendix 4
Further reading

The Edgeless University: Why higher education must embrace technology, 2009, P. Bradwell, Demos, www.demos.co.uk/publications/the-edgeless-university

The Future of Research, 2010, Universities UK

High Growth Firms in Scotland, June 2010, C Mason and R Brown, Hunter Centre for Entrepreneurship, University of Strathclyde and Scottish Enterprise

Higher Ambition: Future of universities in the knowledge economy, 2009, Department for Business Innovation and Skills. Executive summary at www.bis.gov.uk/assets/biscore/corporate/docs/h/09-1452-higher-ambitions-summary.pdf

Higher Education Business and Community Interaction Survey, 2009–10, Higher Education Statistical Agency; www.hesa.ac.uk

Higher education in facts and figures, 2011, Universities UK; www.universitiesuk.ac.uk

Innovation Report, 2010, Department for Business Innovation and Skills/NESTA; www.bis.gov.uk

Knowledge Exchange: Insider special report in association with Interface, 2010; www.interface-online.org.uk or www.business7.co.uk/insider-magazine

Lambert Review of Business-University Collaboration, 2003, HM Treasury; www.hm-treasury.gov.uk/d/lambert_review_final_450.pdf

New Light on Innovation, 2006, Engineering Employers Federation; www.eef.org.uk

Reports on Intellectual Property and Research Benefits for the Secretary of State for Innovation, Universities and Skills, September 2008, Professor Paul Wellings, Lancaster University

Stepping Higher: Workforce development through employer-higher education partnerships, 2008, CBI; www.cbi.org.uk

(Un)common Ground: Creative encounters across sectors and disciplines, 2007, Virtueel Platform; wwww.virtueelplatform.nl

Understanding Work-based Learning, 2010, edited by Simon Roodhouse & John Mumford, Gower

The Wider Conditions for Innovation in the UK: How the UK compares to leading innovation nations, 2009, NESTA; www.nesta.org.uk

Index of advertisers